FILET CRO

ONDORI

CONTENTS

★ Published by Ondorisha Publishers, Ltd.,
  32 Nishigoken-cho, Shinjuku-ku, Tokyo 162, Japan.
★ Sole Overseas Distributors: Japan Publications Trading Co., Ltd.,
  P. O. Box 5030 Tokyo International, Tokyo, Japan.
★ Distributed in the United States by Kodansha International/USA, Ltd.
  through Harper & Row, Publishers, Inc., 10 East 53rd Street, New York,
  New York 10022.

10 9 8 7 6 5 4 3 2 1

★ ISBN 0-87040-559-4 Printed in Japan

Attractive Table Centers

Instructions on page 33. (66 cm in diameter)

1

Instructions on page 34. (80 cm by 41 cm)

(Top) Instructions on page 36. (89 cm by 41.5 cm)

(Bottom) Instructions on page 38. (45 cm by 30 cm)

Instructions on page 38. (74 cm in diameter)

(Top) Instructions on page 40. (73.5 cm by 41 cm)

(Bottom) Instructions on page 41. (82 cm by 49.5 cm)

Instructions on page 42. (112 cm by 87 cm)

(Top) Instructions on page 44. (53 cm by 33 cm)

(Bottom) Instructions on page 44. (113 cm by 33 cm)

Gorgeous Tablecloths

Instructions on page 48. (95 cm square)

Instructions on page 49. (112 cm square)

Instructions on page 54.

(144 cm in diameter)

Instructions on page 52. (108 cm by 99 cm)

Lovely Laces

(Top) Instructions on page 56. (27 cm in diameter)

14   (Bottom) Instructions on page 57. (24 cm square)

(Tray mat) Instructions on page 58. (37 cm by 18.5 cm)

(Coasters) Instructions on page 58. (11 cm squares for A, B, C, D. 12 cm in diameter for E)

(Double square doily) Instructions on page 62. (19 cm square)

(Lace edgings) Instructions on page 60. (2 cm—7.5 cm wide)

(Butterfly doily) Instructions on page 62. (43 cm by 16 cm)

White Accents

Instructions on page 64. (53 cm in diameter)

Instructions on page 65. (44 cm square)

Instructions on page 67. (48 cm square)

Instructions on page 70. (88 cm by 71 cm for large, 43.5 cm by 71 cm for small)

Instructions on page 69. (152 cm by 61 cm for large, 50 cm by 61 cm for small)

(Top) Instructions on page 74. (143 cm by 29.5 cm)

(Bottom) Instructions on page 71. (162 cm by 77.5 cm)

SWEET DREAMS

Instructions on page 78.
(259.5 cm by 177 cm)

Instructions on page 83. (Lace, 8.5 cm wide)

Instructions on page 79. (300 cm by 174 cm)

Elegant Laces

(Top) Instructions on page 84. (54 cm by 28 cm)

(Bottom) Instructions on page 85. (34.5 cm square)

(Top) Instructions on page 86. (34 cm square)

(Bottom) Instructions on page 87. (63.5 cm by 38 cm)

(Top) Instructions on page 88. (84.5 cm by 60.5 cm)

(Bottom) Instructions on page 89. (85.5 cm by 35.5 cm)

DIRECTIONS

All pieces in this book are worked from charts of stitch symbols and patterns rather than from row by row directions.

Spaces are shown on the charts as open squares, blocks as colored squares.

To make one space: Dc in st, ch 2, skip 2 sts, dc in next st.

To make one block: Dc in each of 4 sts.

Round Table Center, shown on page 1.

MATERIALS: Mercerized crochet cotton, No. 30, 150 g white. Steel crochet hook, size 0.90 mm.

FINISHED SIZE: 66 cm in diameter.

GAUGE: 1 dc = 0.4 cm.

DIRECTIONS: Beginning at center, ch 8, join with sl st to form ring. Rnd 1: Ch 7 (d tr 1, ch 2) 15 times in ring, end with sl st. Rnds 2–60: Following chart, work in filet crochet, making flower pattern (A) and butterfly pattern (B) alternately to shape octagon. Cut off thread. Row 61: Attach thread at each corner (8 corners altogether). Work through Row 70, following chart and turning each row. After adding supplementary arch to each edge, work 4 rnd edging all around.

Diagram

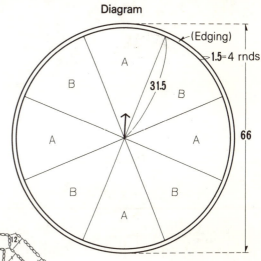

Beginning and Increasing

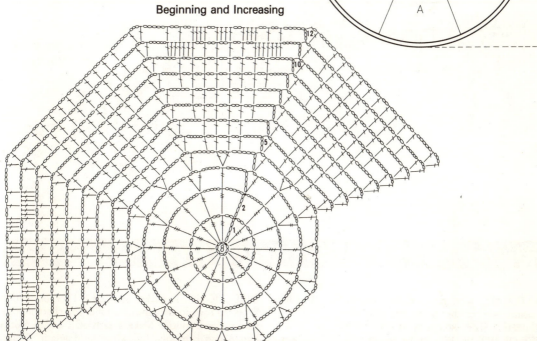

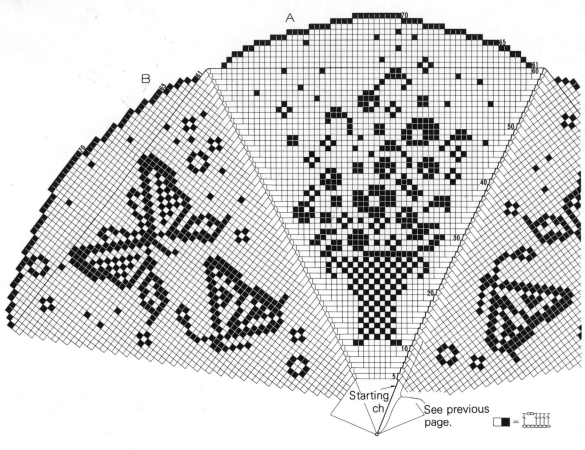

Starting ch

See previous page.

☐■ = ⌶⌶⌶⌶

Decreasing and Edging

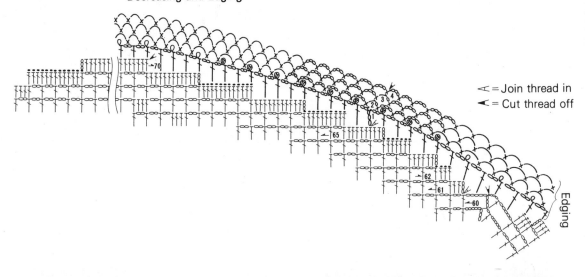

◁ = Join thread in
◀ = Cut thread off

Edging

Chrysanthemum Table Center, shown on page 2.

MATERIALS: Mercerized crochet cotton, No. 30, 140 g white. Steel crochet hook, size 0.90 mm.
FINISHED SIZE: 80 cm by 41 cm.
SIZE OF MOTIF: 17.5 cm by 16 cm.
GAUGE: 10 cm = 23 spaces or blocks; 10 cm = 25 rows.

DIRECTIONS: To make motif, ch 121 for foundation. Work 30 rows in filet crochet, following chart. Reverse pattern for B-motifs. Make 4 each of A and B motifs. Join A and B motifs, following the diagram. Work 8 rnd edging all around.

Diagram

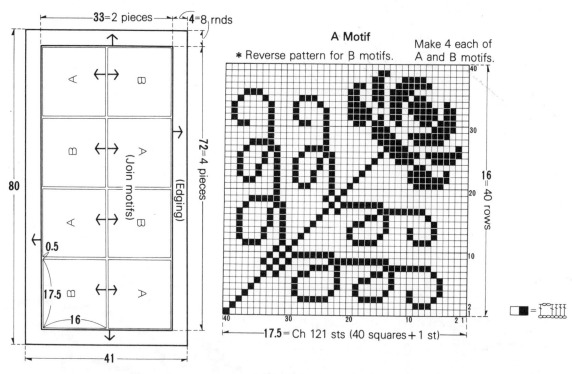

33=2 pieces   **4**=8 rnds

80   72=4 pieces   (Edging)

A   B
B   A (Join motifs)
A   B
B   A

0.5
17.5
16
41

A Motif

* Reverse pattern for B motifs.

Make 4 each of A and B motifs.

16 = 40 rows

17.5=Ch 121 sts (40 squares + 1 st)

Joining Motifs and Edging

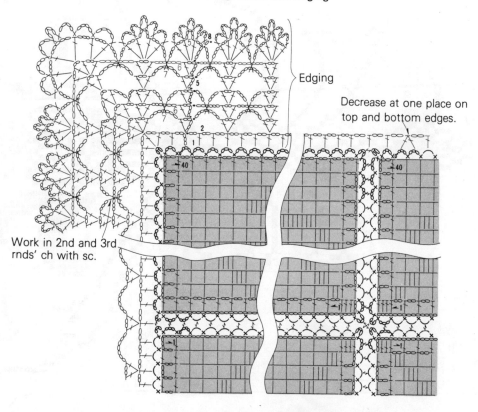

Edging

Decrease at one place on top and bottom edges.

Work in 2nd and 3rd rnds' ch with sc.

MATERIALS: Mercerized crochet cotton, No. 30, 120
g white. Steel crochet hook, size 0.90 mm.
FINISHED SIZE: 89 cm by 41.5 cm.
GAUGE: 10 cm = 21 spaces or blocks; 10 cm = 22 rows.
DIRECTIONS: Ch 244 for foundation. Work 190 rows
in filet crochet, following chart. Work 6 rnd edging all
around.

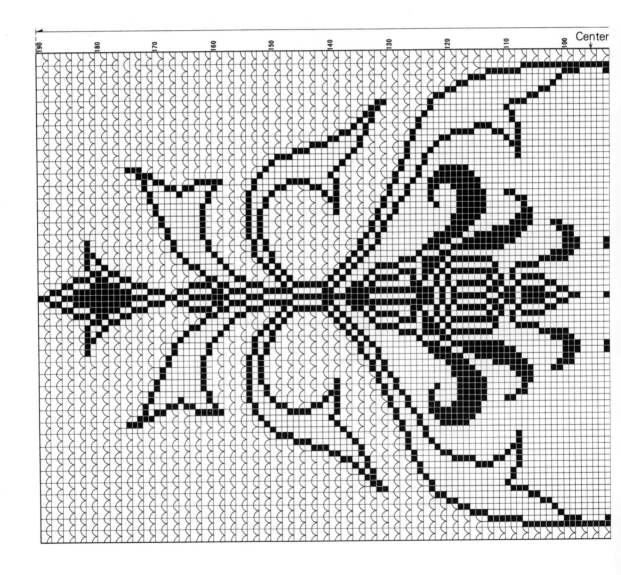

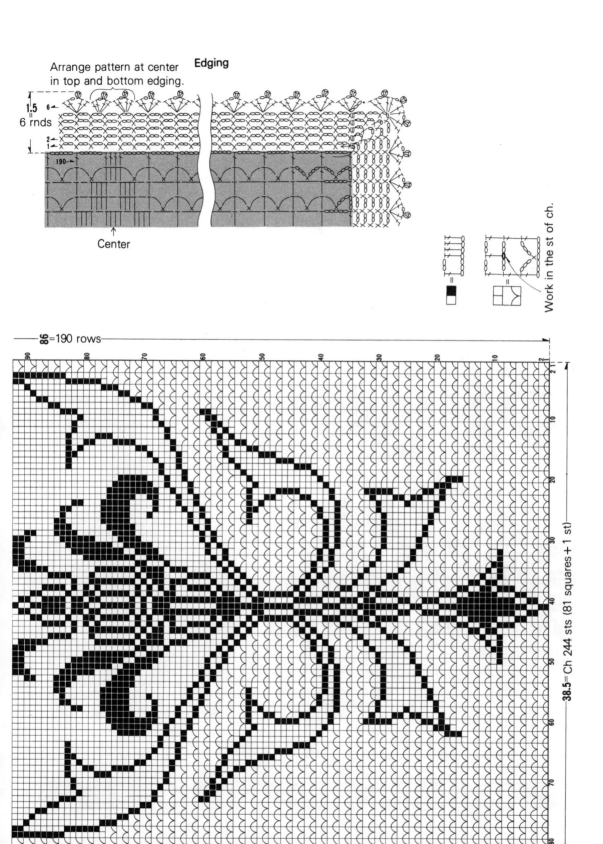

Arrange pattern at center
in top and bottom edging.

Edging

1.5
6 rnds

Center

Work in the st of ch.

86=190 rows

38.5= Ch 244 sts (81 squares + 1 st)

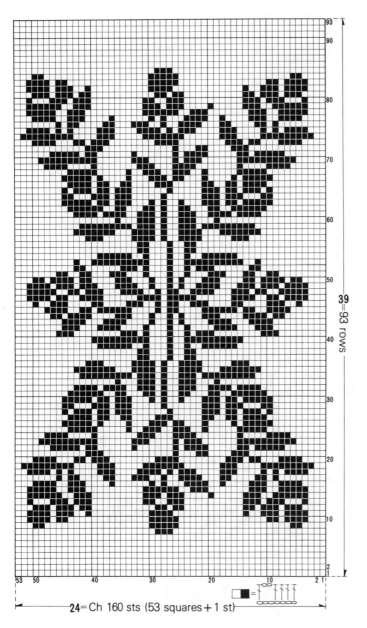

24 = Ch 160 sts (53 squares + 1 st)

MATERIALS: Mercerized crochet cotton, No. 30, 55 g white. Steel crochet hook, size 0.90 mm.
FINISHED SIZE: 45 cm by 30 cm.
GAUGE: 10 cm = 22 spaces or blocks; 10 cm = 24 rows.
DIRECTIONS: Ch 160 for foundation. Work 93 rows in filet crochet, following chart. Work 7 rnd edging all around.

Edging

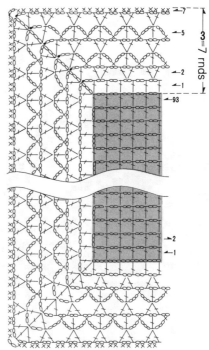

MATERIALS: Mercerized crochet cotton, No. 30, 140 g white. Steel crochet hook, size 0.90 mm.
FINISHED SIZE: 74 cm in diameter.
GAUGE: 1 dc = 0.6 cm.
DIRECTIONS: Beginning at center, ch 12, join with sl

st to form ring. Rnd 1: Ch 4, dc 4, (ch 2, dc 5) 7 times in ring, ch 2, end with sl st. Rnds 2 – 6: Work following chart. Rnds 7–53 ⊖ Ψορχ ιν φιλετ ϑροϑηετ, φολλοψ-ινγ ϑηαρτ ανδ ινϑρεασινγ ατ ειγητ ϑορνερς το μαχε οϑταγον. 3 ρνδ εδγινγ αλλ αρουνδ.

Edging

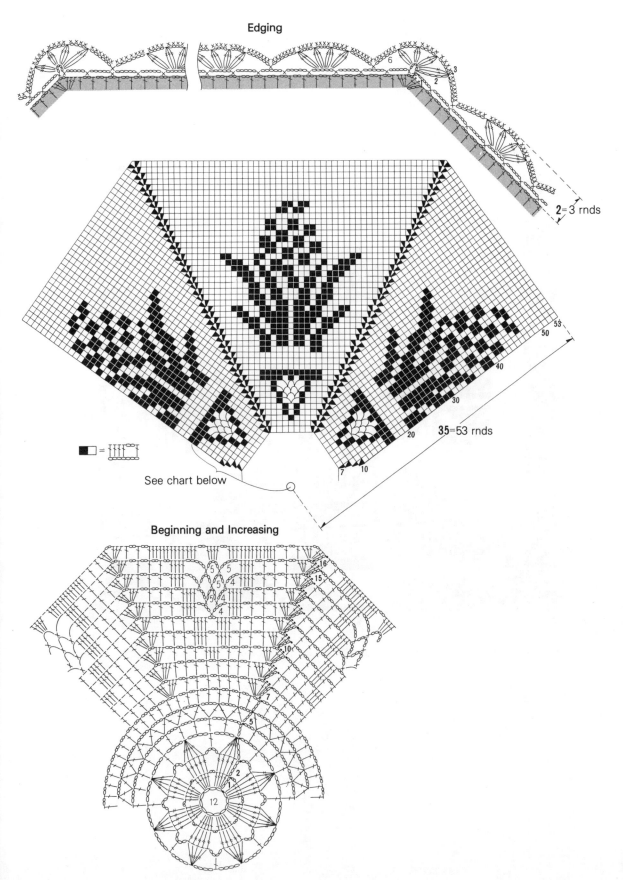

2= 3 rnds

35=53 rnds

■□ = ⫯⫯⫯

See chart below

Beginning and Increasing

Dandelion Table Center, shown on page 5, top.

MATERIALS: Mercerized crochet cotton, No. 30, 110 g white. Steel crochet hook, size 1.00 mm.
FINISHED SIZE: 73.5 cm by 41 cm.
GAUGE: 10 cm = 18.5 spaces or blocks; 10 cm = 18 rows.

DIRECTIONS: Ch 226 for foundation. Work in filet crochet, following chart. Reverse pattern for other half. Work 3 rnd edging all around.

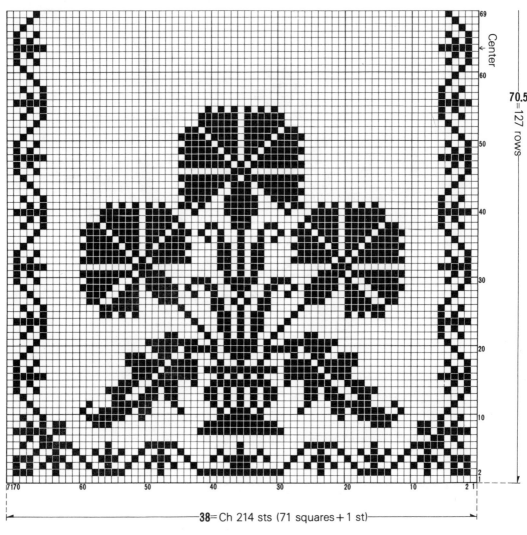

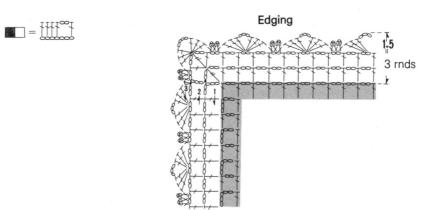

Edging

1.5 = 3 rnds

Fish Table Center, shown on page 5, bottom.

MATERIALS: Mercerized crochet cotton, No. 30, 90 g white. Steel crochet hook, size 0.90 mm.

FINISHED SIZE: 82 cm by 49.5 cm.

GAUGE: 10 cm = 13.5 spaces or blocks; 10 cm = 13.5 rows.

DIRECTIONS: Ch 241 for foundation. Work 104 rows in filet crochet and lacet stitches, following chart. Work 3 rnd edging all around.

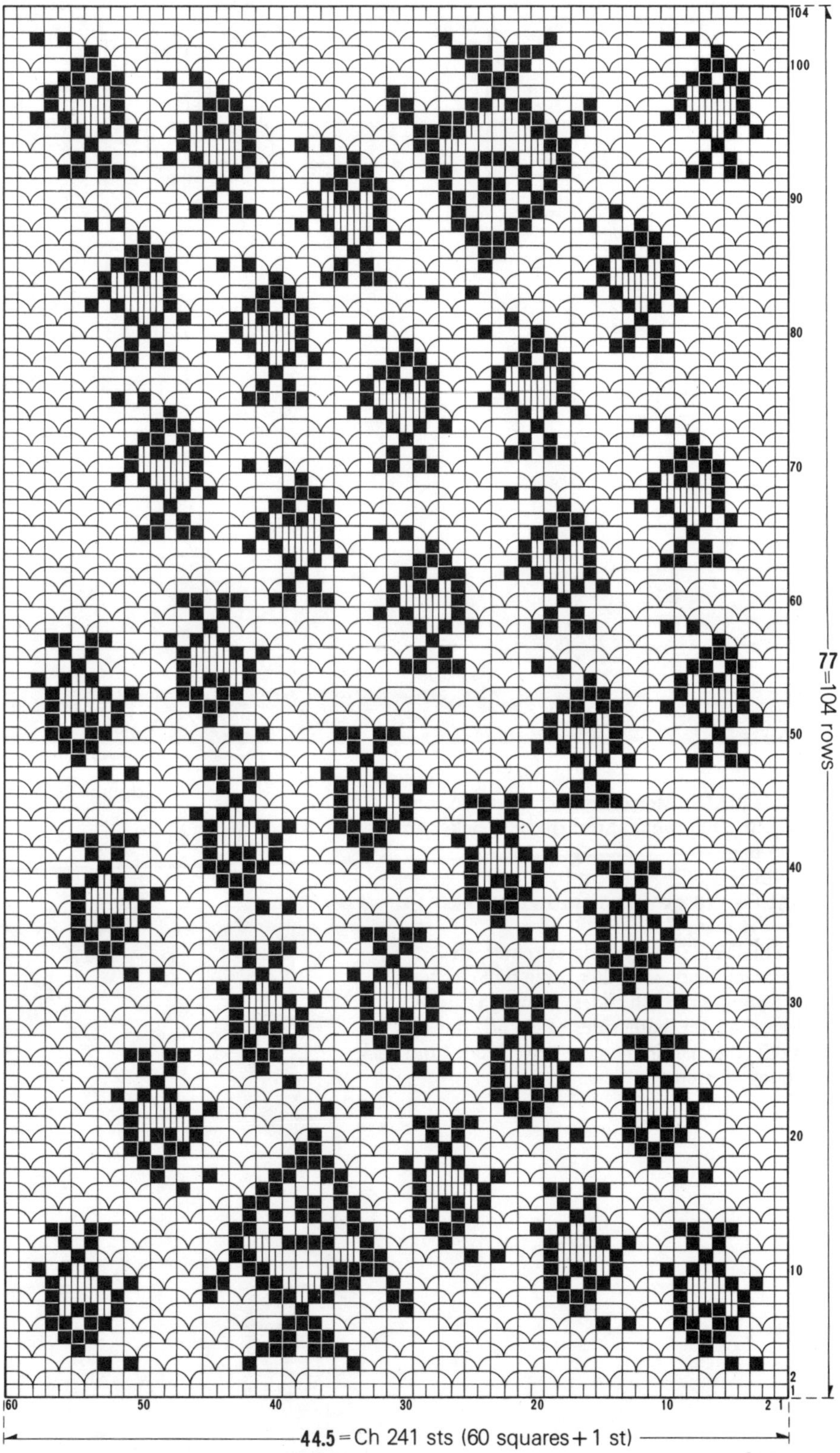

= Tr in ch.

77 = 104 rows

44.5 = Ch 241 sts (60 squares + 1 st)

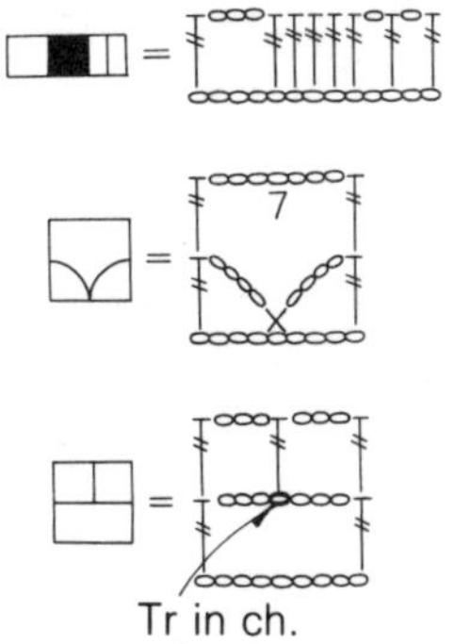

(Edging shown on next page)

41

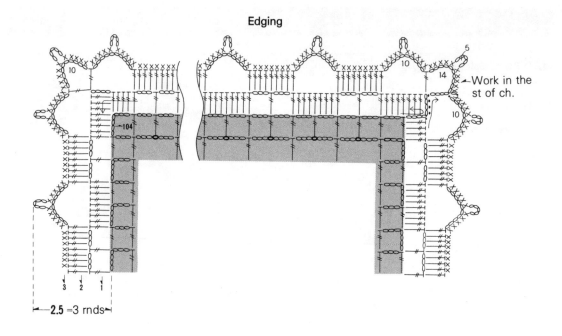

Edging

→ Work in the st of ch.

10   5

14

10

104

3 2 1

2.5 = 3 rnds

Iris Table Center, shown on page 6.

MATERIALS: Mercerized crochet cotton, No. 30, 170 g white. Steel crochet hook, size 0.90 mm.

FINISHED SIZE: 112 cm by 87 cm.

GAUGE: 10 cm = 13.5 spaces or blocks; 10 cm = 15 rows.

DIRECTIONS: Beginning at center, ch 261. Following chart, work 26 rows in filet crochet, increasing on both sides. Work 57 rows, decreasing on both sides. Cut off thread. Work other half in the same way. Work 1 rnd edging all around.

Edging

Cut thread off.

1   9

57

1 = 1 rnd

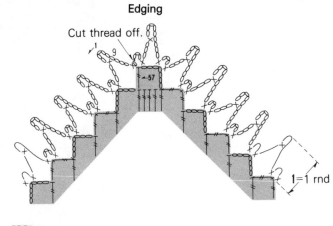

2

1

2

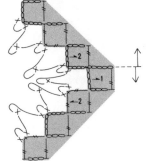

38 = 57 rows — 17.5 = 26 rows — 16.5 = 25 rows

18.5 = 25 squares

← Center

18.5 = 25 squares

48 = Ch 261 sts (65 squares + 1 st)

Decreasing

Increasing

Join thread in

Ch 261 sts

Tr in ch.

MATERIALS: Mercerized crochet cotton, No. 30, 60 g white. Steel crochet hook, size 0.90 mm.
FINISHED SIZE: 53 cm by 33 cm.
SIZE OF MOTIF: 10 cm square.
GAUGE: 2 dc = 1.1 cm.
DIRECTIONS: Make loop at end of thread. Rnd 1: Ch 5, (dc 1, ch 4 dc 1, ch 2) 3 times, dc 1, ch 2, end with h dc. All dc sts are inserted into loop. Rnds 2–9: Work in filet crochet following chart. Make 2nd motif in the same way and join to 1st motif in the 9th rnd with sl st. Make and join 5 by 3 motifs. Work 3 rnd edging all around.

Diagram

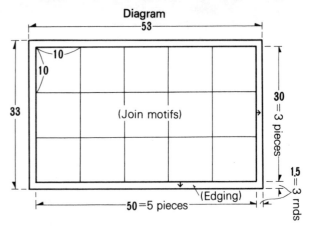

Motif and Edging

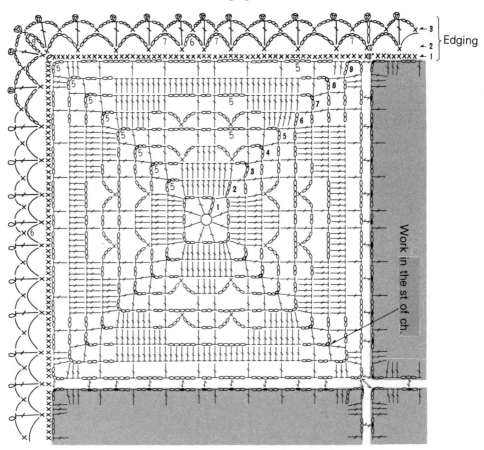

MATERIALS: Mercerized crochet cotton, No. 40, 130 g white. Steel crochet hook, size 0.90 mm.
FINISHED SIZE: 113 cm by 33 cm.

SIZE OF MOTIF: 9.5 cm square.
GAUGE: 9.5 cm = 19 spaces or blocks; 9.5 cm = 19 rows.

A motif   Make 22 pieces.

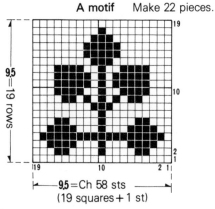

9,5=19 rows

9,5=Ch 58 sts
(19 squares + 1 st)

B motif   Make 11 pieces.

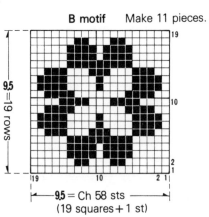

9,5=19 rows

9,5 = Ch 58 sts
(19 squares + 1 st)

DIRECTIONS: To make A or B motif, ch 58 for foundation. Work 18 rows in filet crochet, following chart. Work 1 rnd in mesh pattern of 3 ch and 1 sc. Make 2nd motif in same way and join to 1st motif with edging. Make and join 22 A-motifs and 11 B-motifs. Work 4 rnd edging all around.

Diagram

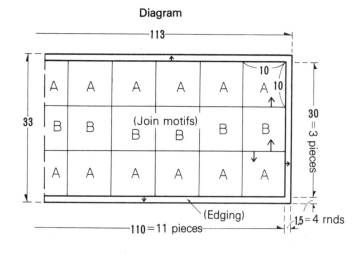

113

33

A	A	A	A	A	A
B	B	(Join motifs) B B		B	B
A	A	A	A	A	A

10
10
30
=3 pieces

(Edging)

110=11 pieces

1,5=4 rnds

Edging and Joining

□■ =

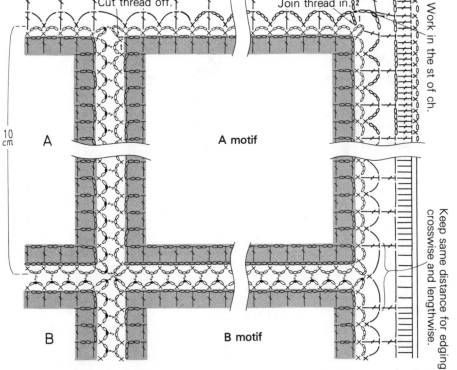

Cut thread off.

Cut thread off.

Join thread in.

A

A motif

B

B motif

10 cm

Work in the st of ch.

Keep same distance for edging crosswise and lengthwise.

MATERIALS: Mercerized crochet cotton, No. 30, 320 g white. Steel crochet hook, size 1.00 mm.
FINISHED SIZE: 112 cm square.
SIZE OF MOTIF: 13.5 cm square.
GAUGE: 10 cm=18.5 spaces or blocks; 10 cm=18.5 rows.
DIRECTIONS: To make 1st motif, ch 76 for foundation. Work 25 rows in filet crochet, following chart. Work 2 rnd edging. Make 2nd motif in the same way and join to 1st motif in the 2nd rnd of edging with sl st.
Make and join 8 A motifs, 17 B motifs and 24 C motifs. Position motifs as indicated by arrows when joining.

Diagram

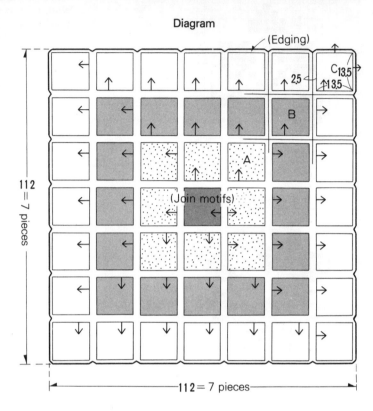

112 = 7 pieces

112 = 7 pieces

A motif   Make 8 pieces

B motif   Make 17 pieces

C motif   Make 24 pieces

13.5 = 25 rows

13.5 = 25 rows

13.5=Ch 76 sts
(25 squares+1 st)

13.5=Ch 76 sts
(25 squares+1 st)

13.5=Ch 76 sts
(25 squares+1 st)

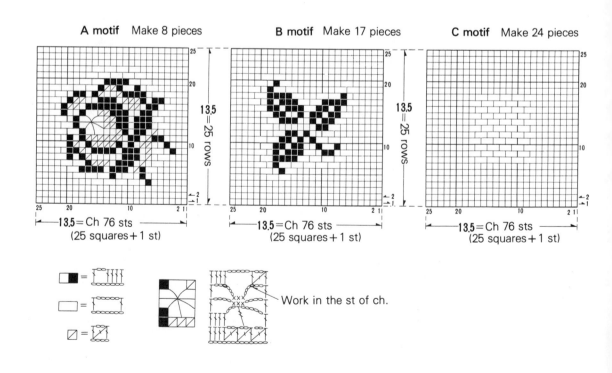

Work in the st of ch.

Joining and Edging

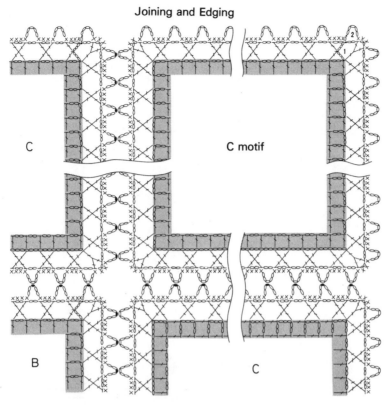

C

C motif

B

C

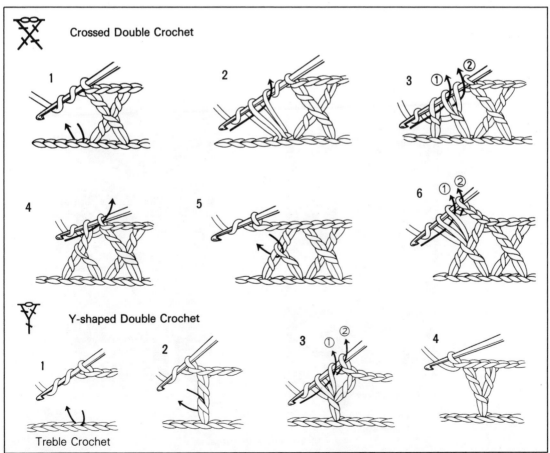

Crossed Double Crochet

1 2 3 ① ②

4 5 6 ① ②

Y-shaped Double Crochet

1 2 3 ① ② 4

Treble Crochet

MATERIALS: Mercerized crochet cotton, No. 30, 360 g whete. Steel crochet hook, size 0.90 mm.
FINISHED SIZE: 95 cm square.
SIZE OF MOTIF: 90 cm by 12 cm.
GAUGE: 10 cm = 20 spaces or blocks; 10 cm = 20.5 rows.
DIRECTIONS: Make A motif first. Ch 73 for foundation. Following chart, work 23 rows in filet crochet, to make one pattern. Make 7 more patterns until piece reaches 185th row. Make 2nd motif in same way, joining to 1st motif with chain loops. Make and join 4 A motifs and 3 B motifs. Work 5 rnd edging all around.

Diagram

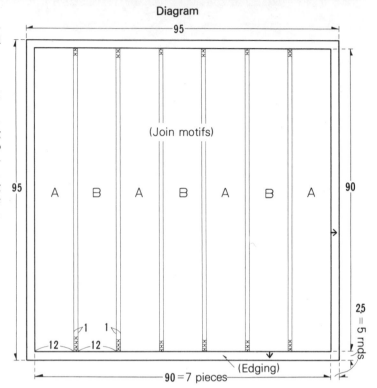

A-motif

B motif

* Make chain loops on one side only for motifs placed on right and left sides.

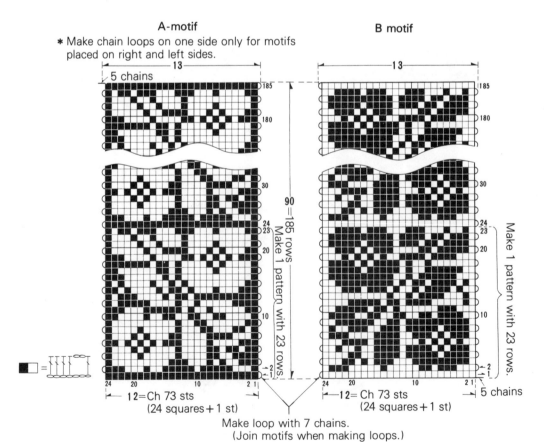

Make loop with 7 chains.
(Join motifs when making loops.)

Motifs and Edging

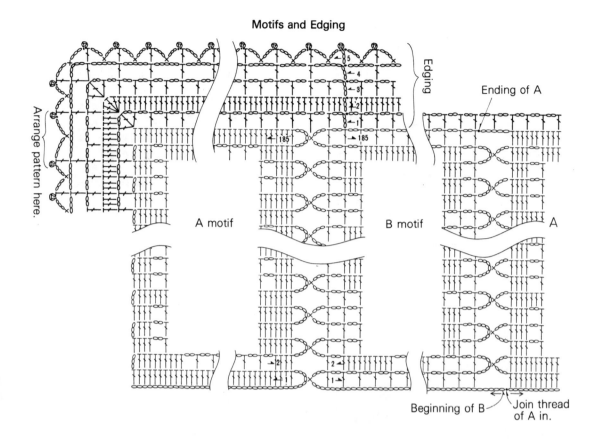

Edging

Ending of A

Arrange pattern here.

A motif

B motif

A

185   185

5
4
3
2
1

2
1

2
1

Beginning of B — Join thread of A in.

Geometric Tablecloth, *shown on page 10.*

MATERIALS: Mercerized crochet cotton, No. 30, 370 g white. Steel crochet hook, size 0.90 mm.
FINISHED SIZE: 112 cm square.
SIZE OF MOTIF: 19 cm square.
GAUGE: 10 cm = 14 spaces or blocks; 10 cm = 14 rows.
DIRECTIONS: To make A or B motif, begin at center and ch 5. Rnd 1: Ch 4, dc 1 in each ch. Rnds 2 – 14: Work in filet crochet, following chart. Work edging (1) all around. Make 2nd motif in the same way and join to 1st motif following the diagram. Make and join 13 A motifs and 12 B motifs. Work edging (2) all around.

Diagram

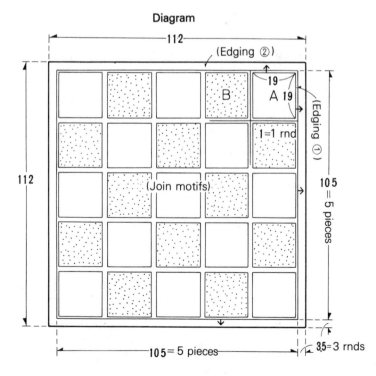

112

(Edging ②)

B

A 19

19

(Edging ①)

1=1 rnd

112

(Join motifs)

105 = 5 pieces

105 = 5 pieces

3.5 = 3 rnds

A motif   Make 13 pieces   B motif   Make 12 pieces

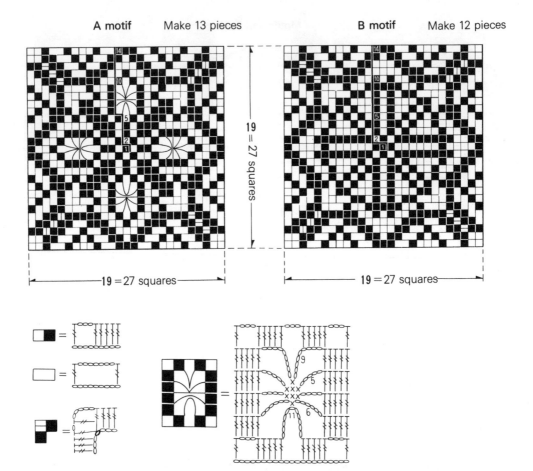

19 = 27 squares

19 = 27 squares

19 = 27 squares

Beginning A motif and corner

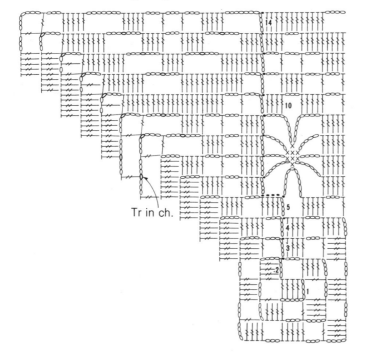

Tr in ch.

Beginning B motif

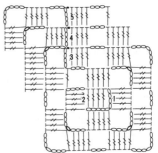

Joinning and Edging

Edging ②

Edging ①

A motif

B

B

A

Tr in ch.

Cut
thread in.   thread off.

Join
thread in.

3.5 = 3 rnds

1 = 1 rnd.

51

MATERIALS: Mercerized crochet cotton, No. 30, 490 g white. Steel crochet hook, size 0.90 mm.
FINISHED SIZE: 108 cm by 99 cm.
GAUGE: 10 cm = 22 spaces or blocks; 10 cm = 24 rows.

DIRECTIONS: Ch 712 for foundation. Work 119 rows in filet crochet, following chart. Work other half until the piece reaches 237th row, reversing pattern. Work sc all around.

108=Ch 712 sts (237 squares + 1 st)

Single Crochet of Edging

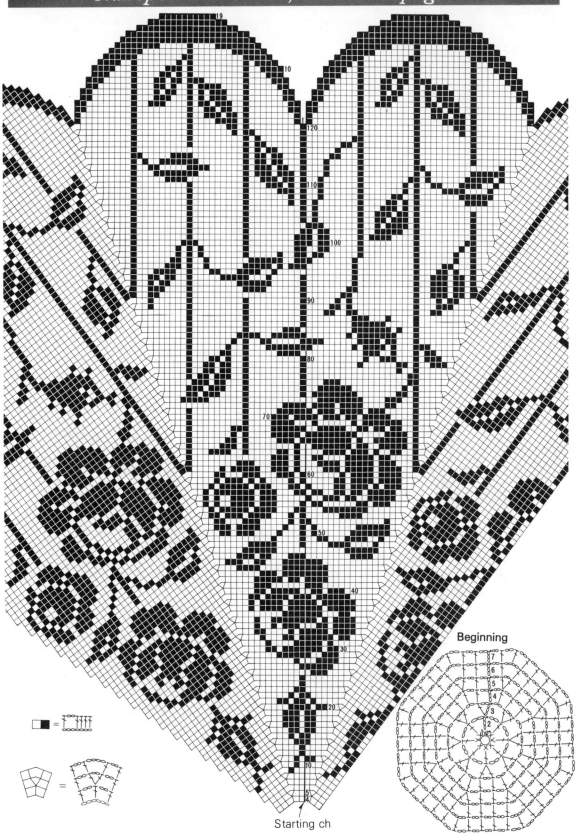

Beginning

Starting ch

MATERIALS: Mercerized crochet cotton, No. 30, 450 g white. Steel crochet hook, size 0.90 mm.
FINISHED SIZE: 144 cm in diameter.
GAUGE: 1 dc = 0.5 cm.
DIRECTIONS: Make loop at end of thread. Rnd 1: Ch 1, sc 8 in loop, end with sl st. Rnds 2–120: Work in filet crochet, following chart. Attach thread at each corner, and work 19 rows to make scallops.

Decreasing

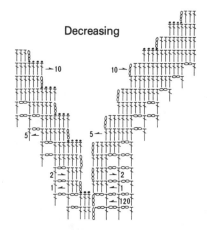

Bird and Tree Doily, shown on page 13.

MATERIALS: Mercerized crochet cotton, No. 30, 40 g beige. Steel crochet hook, size 0.90 mm.
FINISHED SIZE: 34 cm in diameter.
GAUGE: 1 dc = 0.5 cm.

DIRECTIONS: Ch 7, join with sl st to form ring. Work 33 rnds in filet crochet, following chart. Work one rnd edging all around.

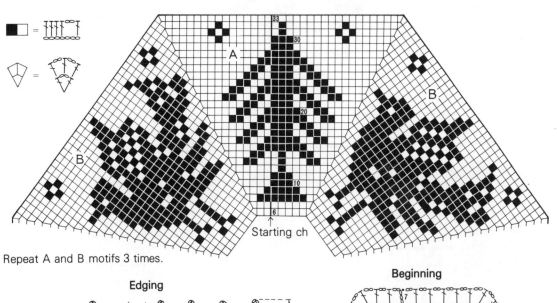

Repeat A and B motifs 3 times.

Edging

Beginning

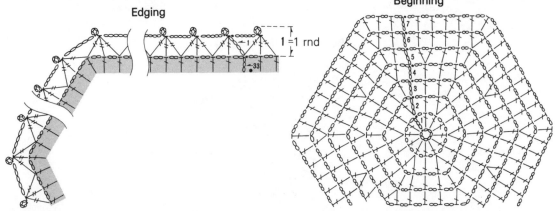

55

MATERIALS: Mercerized crochet cotton, No. 30, 25 g white. Steel crochet hook, size 0.90 mm.
FINISHED SIZE: 27 cm in diameter.
GAUGE: 2 dc = 0.9 cm.
DIRECTIONS: Make loop at end of thread. Rnd 1: Ch

3, (ch 1, dc 1) 11 times in loop, end with sl st. Rnds 2–23: Work in filet crochet following chart and increasing at six corners. Attach thread at each corner and work 7 rows to make scallops.

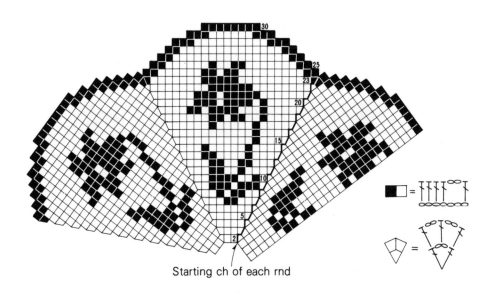

Starting ch of each rnd

Decreasing

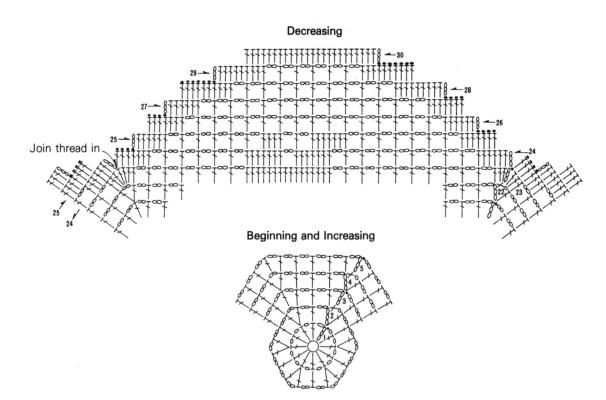

Join thread in

Beginning and Increasing

Square Doily, shown on page 14, bottom.

MATERIALS: Mercerized crochet cotton, No. 30, 20 g white. Steel crochet hook, size 0.90 mm.
FINISHED SIZE: 24 cm square.

GAUGE: 10 cm = 21 spaces or blocks; 10 cm = 21 rows.
DIRECTIONS: Ch 142 for foundation. Work 47 rows in filet crochet, following chart. Work 2 rnd edging.

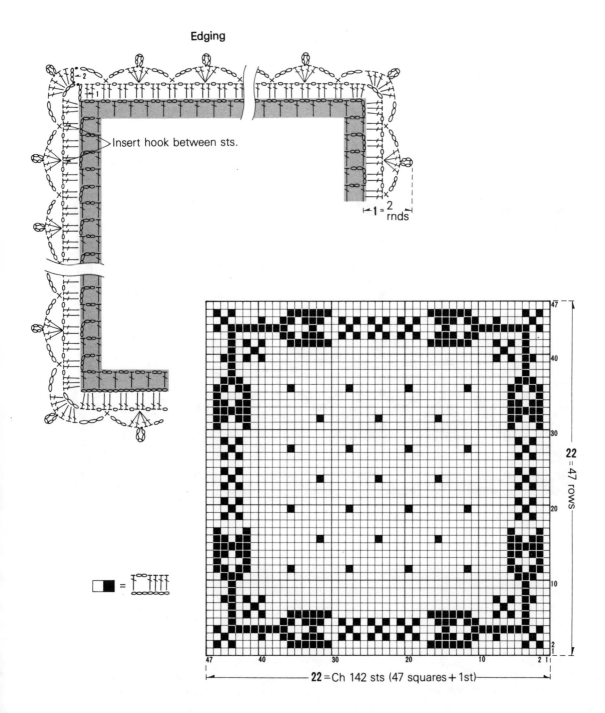

Edging

Insert hook between sts.

1 = 2 rnds

=

22 = 47 rows

22 = Ch 142 sts (47 squares + 1st)

MATERIALS: Mercerized crochet cotton, No. 30, 30 g white. Steel crochet hook, size 0.90 mm.
FINISHED SIZE: 37 cm by 18.5 cm.
GAUGE: 10 cm = 19.5 spaces or blocks; 10 cm = 24 rows.
DIRECTIONS: Ch 205 for foundation. Work 40 rows in filet crochet, following chart. Work 2 rnd edging.

Edging

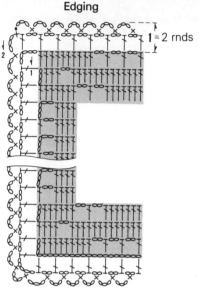

1 = 2 rnds

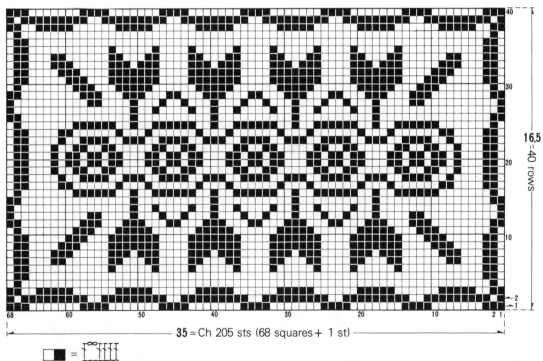

35 = Ch 205 sts (68 squares + 1 st)

16,5 = 40 rows

MATERIALS: Mercerized crochet cotton, No. 30, small amount of white. Steel crochet hook, size 0.90 mm.
FINISHED SIZE: A – D: 11 cm square each. E: 12 cm in diameter.
GAUGE: A – D: 10 cm = 21 spaces or blocks; 10 cm = 21 rows. E: 1 dc = 0.5 cm.

DIRECTIONS: FOR A – D: Make foundation chain as indicated. Work in filet crochet, following each chart. For C and D, increase or decrease in the same way as for A.
FOR E: Make loop at end of thread. Rnd 1: Ch 3, (ch 2, dc 1) 11 times in loop, ch 2, end with sl st. Rnds 2 – 13: Work in filet crochet, following chart.

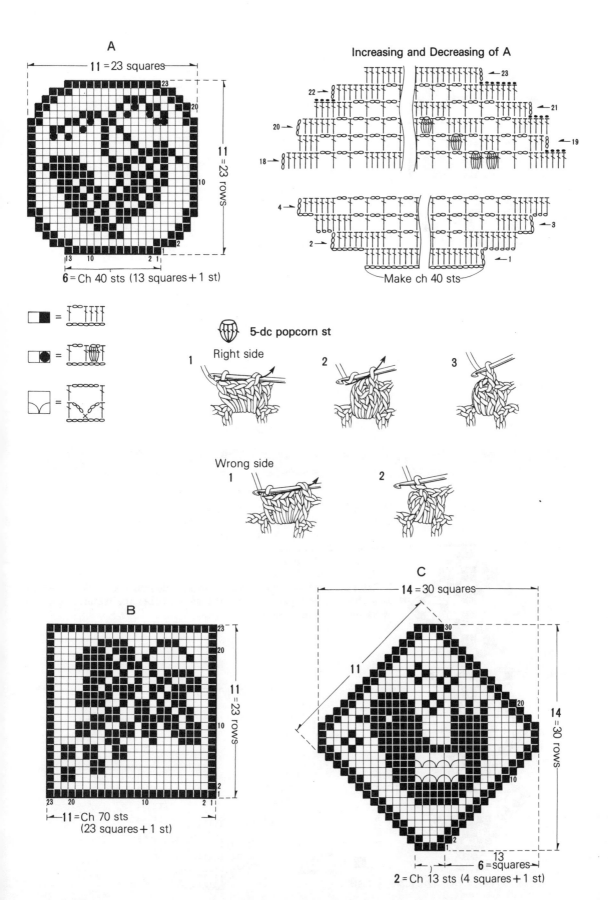

A

11 = 23 squares

11 = 23 rows

10

6 = Ch 40 sts (13 squares + 1 st)

Increasing and Decreasing of A

Make ch 40 sts

= 5-dc popcorn st

Right side

1   2   3

Wrong side

1   2

B

11 = 23 rows

10

11 = Ch 70 sts
(23 squares + 1 st)

C

14 = 30 squares

11

14 = 30 rows

20

10

13 squares

6 = squares

2 = Ch 13 sts (4 squares + 1 st)

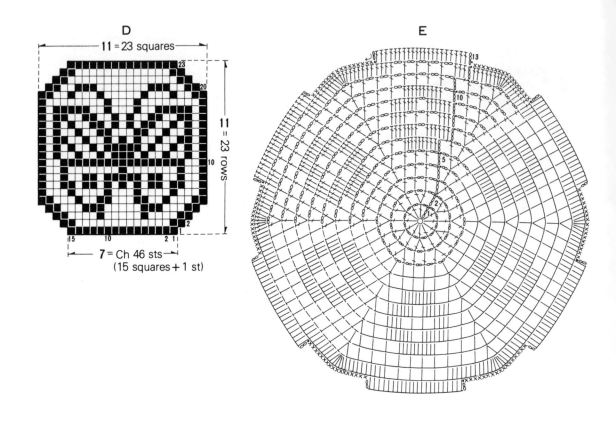

D

11 = 23 squares

11 = 23 rows

10

23
20

15 10 2 1

7 = Ch 46 sts
(15 squares + 1 st)

E

13

10

5

2

Lace Edging, shown on pages 16 and 17.

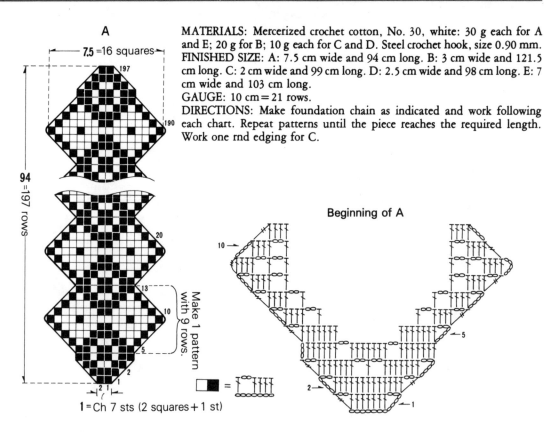

A

7.5 = 16 squares

94 = 197 rows

197

190

20

13

10

5

2

Make 1 pattern with 9 rows.

2   1

1 = Ch 7 sts (2 squares + 1 st)

MATERIALS: Mercerized crochet cotton, No. 30, white: 30 g each for A and E; 20 g for B; 10 g each for C and D. Steel crochet hook, size 0.90 mm.
FINISHED SIZE: A: 7.5 cm wide and 94 cm long. B: 3 cm wide and 121.5 cm long. C: 2 cm wide and 99 cm long. D: 2.5 cm wide and 98 cm long. E: 7 cm wide and 103 cm long.
GAUGE: 10 cm = 21 rows.
DIRECTIONS: Make foundation chain as indicated and work following each chart. Repeat patterns until the piece reaches the required length. Work one rnd edging for C.

Beginning of A

10

5

2

1

B

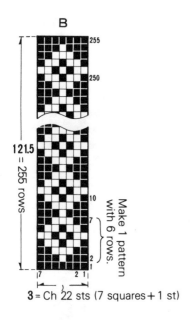

255

250

10

7

2
1

7   2 1

121.5 = 255 rows

Make 1 pattern with 6 rows.

3 = Ch 22 sts (7 squares + 1 st)

C

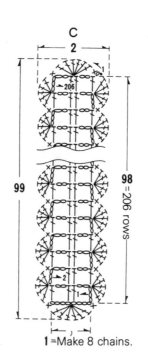

2

206

99

98 = 206 rows

2

1 = Make 8 chains.

D

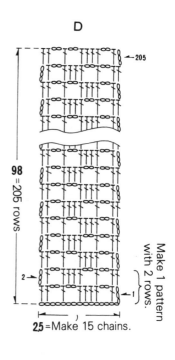

205

98 = 205 rows

2

1

Make 1 pattern with 2 rows.

2.5 = Make 15 chains.

E

7 = 15 squares

217

210

20

12

10

2

10   2 1

103 = 217 rows

Make 1 pattern with 12 rows.

4.5 = Ch 31 sts (10 squares + 1 st)

☐ ■ =

Beginning of E

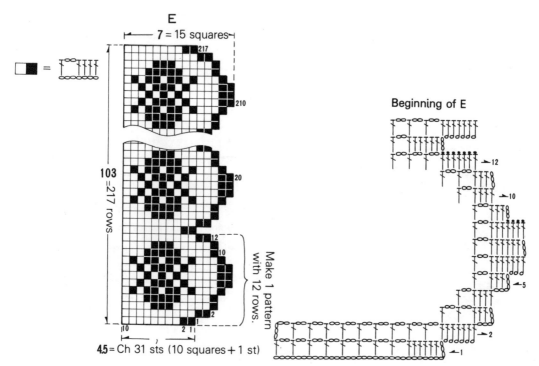

12

10

5

2

1

MATERIALS: Mercerized crochet cotton, No. 30, 10 g white. Steel crochet hook, size 0.90 mm.
FINISHED SIZE: 19 cm by 19 cm.
GAUGE: 10 cm = 21 rows.
DIRECTIONS: Ch 13 for foundation. Work 40 rows in filet crochet, following chart. See chart for increasing and decreasing.

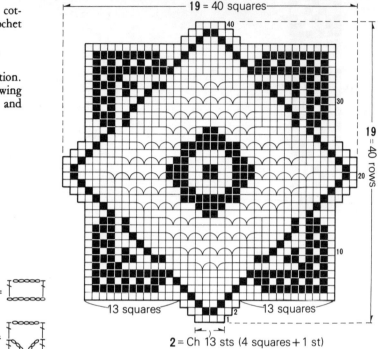

2 = Ch 13 sts (4 squares + 1 st)

Decreasing

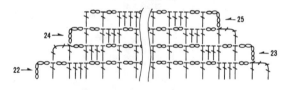

Beginning and Increasing

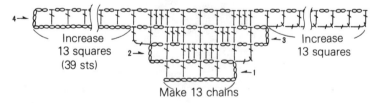

MATERIALS: Mercerized crochet cotton, No. 30, 25 g white. Steel crochet hook, size 0.90 mm.
FINISHED SIZE: 43 cm by 16 cm.
GAUGE: 10 cm = 20 spaces or blocks; 10 cm = 22 rows.

DIRECTIONS: Ch 169 for foundation. Work 34 rows in filet crochet, following chart. On 35th row, work in sl st and ch as shown in Fig. A.

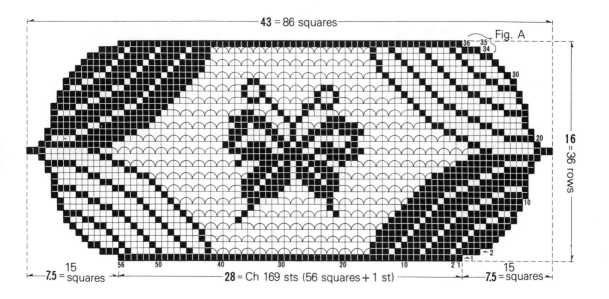

43 = 86 squares

Fig. A

16 = 36 rows

15
7.5 = squares

28 = Ch 169 sts (56 squares + 1 st)

15
7.5 = squares

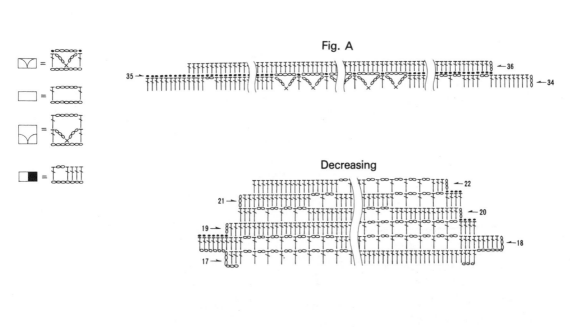

Fig. A

Decreasing

Beginning and Increasing

Make 169 chains

9 chains

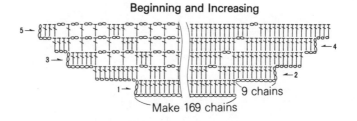

MATERIALS FOR ONE PILLOW: Mercerized crochet cotton, No. 30, 130 g white. Steel crochet hook, size 0.90 mm. Yellow-green (light green) cotton fabric, 55 cm by 110 cm. Kapok, 600 g.

FINISHED SIZE: 53 cm in diameter.

GAUGE: 2 dc = 1.1 cm.

DIRECTIONS: For Front: Make loop at end of thread. Rnd 1: Ch 3, dc 23 in loop, end with sl st. Rnds 2 – 48: Work in filet crochet, following chart and increasing at 12 places on each rnd. For Back: Work in the same way as for Front through Rnd 4. Rnd 5 – 48: Work in filet crochet of (dc 1, ch 2), increasing in the same way as for Rnds 12 – 15. With wrong sides of FRONT and BACK facing, sc together. Before completely closed, insert inner pillow (make 53 cm-diameter inner pillow with cotton fabric and stuff with kapok), and finish.

Front

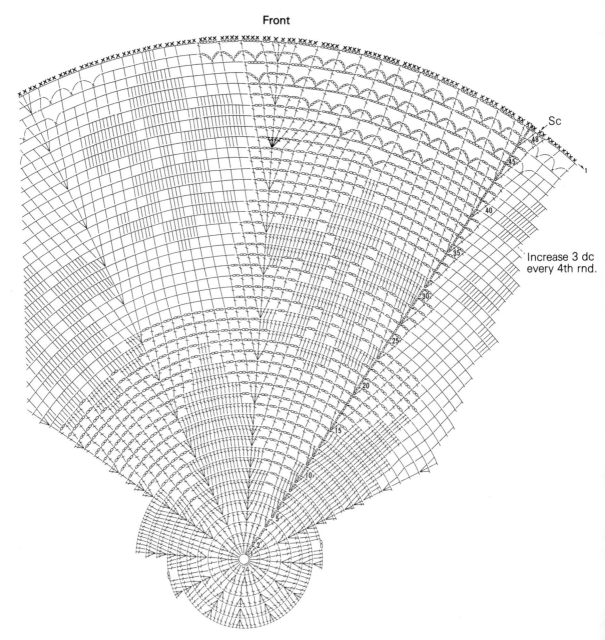

Sc

Increase 3 dc every 4th rnd.

Back

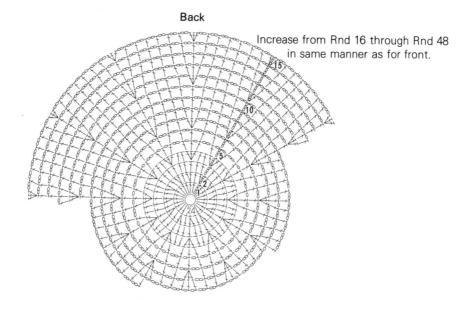

Increase from Rnd 16 through Rnd 48
in same manner as for front.

Square Pillows, shown on page 19.

MATERIALS FOR ONE PILLOW: Mercerized crochet cotton, No. 30, 140 g white. Steel crochet hook, size 1.00 mm. Dark brown bemberg silk, 90 cm by 46 cm. Inner pillow stuffed with kapok, 45 cm square. White satin ribbon, 0.6 cm by 100 cm.

FINISHED SIZE: 44 cm square.
SIZE OF MOTIF: 20 cm square.
GAUGE: 10 cm = 22 spaces or blocks; 10 cm = 22 rows.

DIRECTIONS: To make motif, ch 133 for foundation. Work 44 rows in filet crochet, following chart. Make and join 4 motifs, with stitches in directions indicated by arrows. Work 3 rnds in filet crochet. Continue to work Back in filet crochet, decreasing as indicated. Make 44 cm square inner pillow with Bemberg silk and stuff with kapok. Cover inner pillow with lace pillow. Insert ribbon into open squares of last rnd and tie knot.

Diagram

13.5
30 rows
1.5=3 rnds

Stitch continuously with matching marks.

20

Front
(Join motifs)

20

1

Back
(Filet crochet)

Insert ribbon into open squares of last rnd.

44

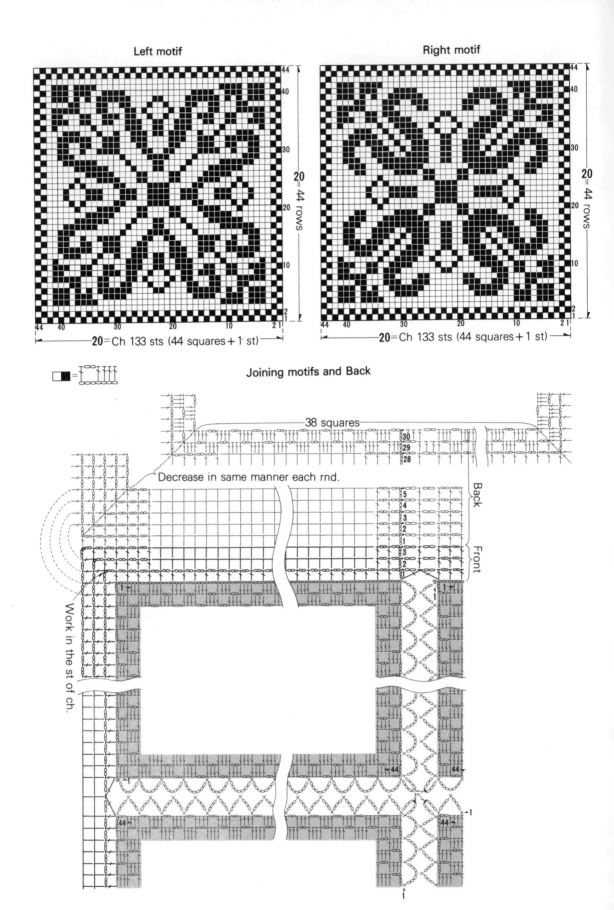

Left motif

Right motif

20 = 44 rows

20 = 44 rows

20 = Ch 133 sts (44 squares + 1 st)

20 = Ch 133 sts (44 squares + 1 st)

Joining motifs and Back

38 squares

Decrease in same manner each rnd.

Back

Front

Work in the st of ch.

Tulip Pillows, shown on page 20.

MATERIALS FOR ONE PILLOW: Mercerized crochet cotton, No. 30, 150 g light blue. Steel crochet hook, sizes 0.90 mm and 1.75 mm. Blue velveteen, 52 cm by 102 cm. Inner pillow stuffed with kapok, 50 cm square.
FINISHED SIZE: 48 cm square.
GAUGE: 10 cm = 20 spaces or blocks; 10 cm = 20 rows.
DIRECTIONS: For Front: Ch 277 for foundation. Work 92 rows in filet crochet, following chart. Work 2 rnds in filet crochet. Then work 4 rows on each side. For Back: Work in mesh pattern of (sc 1, ch 8), decreasing at corners as indicated. Make chain braid with tassels on each end. Insert braid into open squares of last rnd. Make 50 cm square inner pillow with velveteen. Sew corners diagonally as shown and stuff with kapok. Cover inner pillow with lace pillow and tie braid.

Front

46 = Ch 277 sts (92 squares + 1 st)

67

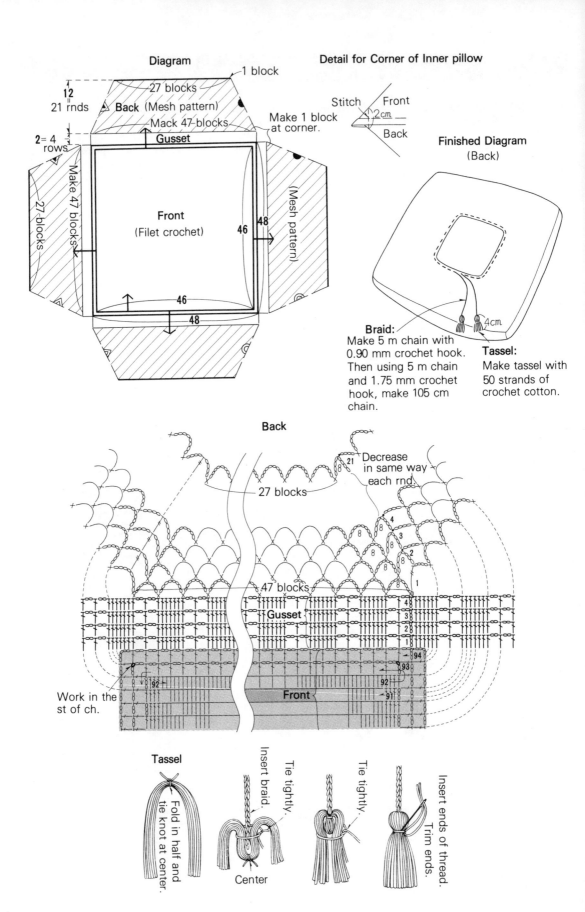

Diagram

1 block

27 blocks

12
21 rnds

Back (Mesh pattern)

Mack 47 blocks

Make 1 block
at corner.

2= 4
rows

Gusset

Make 47 blocks

27 blocks

Front
(Filet crochet)

(Mesh pattern)

46

48

46

48

Detail for Corner of Inner pillow

Stitch   Front

2cm

Back

Finished Diagram
(Back)

4cm

Braid:
Make 5 m chain with
0.90 mm crochet hook.
Then using 5 m chain
and 1.75 mm crochet
hook, make 105 cm
chain.

Tassel:
Make tassel with
50 strands of
crochet cotton.

Back

Decrease
in same way
each rnd

21

27 blocks

4

8   8

8   3

8

2

8

47 blocks

1

Gusset

4
3
2
1

94

93

92

92

Front

91

Work in the
st of ch.

Tassel

Fold in half and
tie knot at center.

Insert braid.

Tie tightly.

Center

Tie tightly.

Insert ends of thread.
Trim ends.

Chair Backs,
shown on page 24.

MATERIALS: Mercerized crochet cotton, No. 30, 320 g for large piece and 110 g for small piece, white. Steel crochet hook, sizes 0.90 mm and 0.75 mm.
FINISHED SIZE: Large: 152 cm by 61 cm. Small: 50 cm by 61 cm.
SIZE OF MOTIF: 61 cm by 16 cm.
GAUGE: 10 cm = 22 spaces or blocks; 10 cm = 24 rows.
DIRECTIONS: To make motif, ch 16 for foundation. Work 6 rows in filet crochet, increasing on both sides until there are 35 squares. Then work even 140 rows in filet crochet, following chart. Make and join 9 motifs for large piece, and 3 motifs for small one as shown in diagram. Work sc all around with 0.75 mm crochet hook.

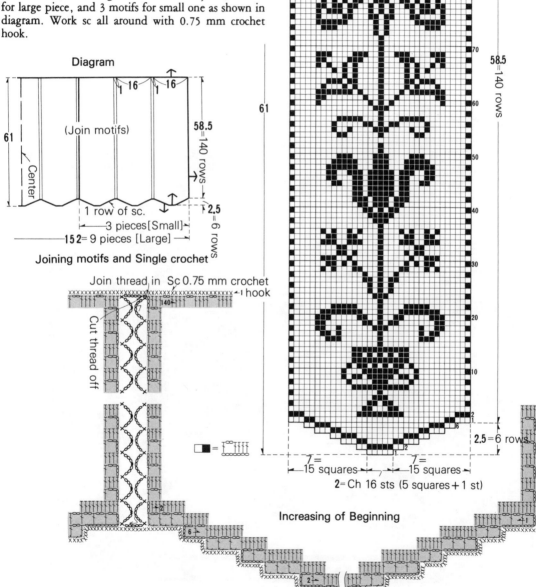

16 = 35 squares

Repeat Rows 97 – 106 for Rows 107 – 136.

58.5 = 140 rows

61

Diagram

(Join motifs)

61   Center

58.5 = 140 rows

1 row of sc.

2.5 = 6 rows

3 pieces [Small]

152 = 9 pieces [Large]

Joining motifs and Single crochet

Join thread in Sc 0.75 mm crochet hook

Cut thread off

=

7 = 15 squares   7 = 15 squares

2 = Ch 16 sts (5 squares + 1 st)

2.5 = 6 rows

Increasing of Beginning

Make 16 chains.

Motif

Make 1 piece for small motif.   Make 2 pieces for large motif.

43.5 = 89 squares

Repeat Rows 83 — 100 for Rows 101 — 118.

65.5 = 137 rows

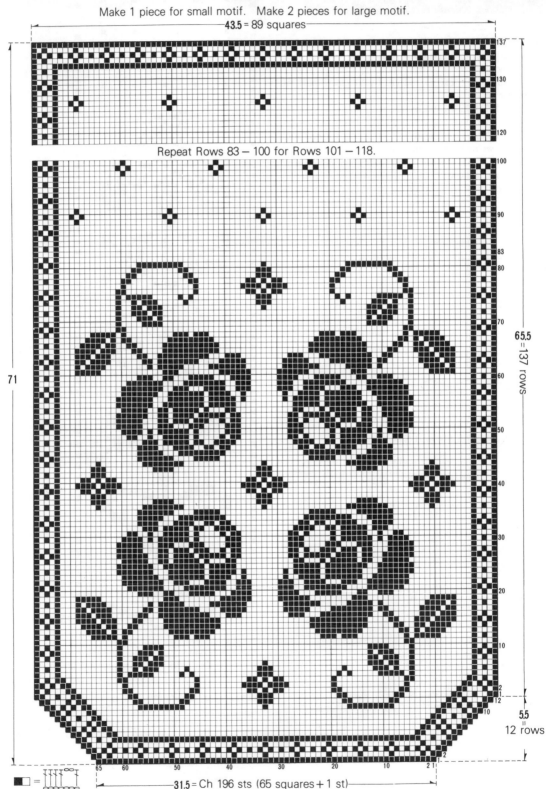

31.5 = Ch 196 sts (65 squares + 1 st)

5.5 = 12 rows

MATERIALS: Mercerized crochet cotton, No. 30, 220 g for large piece and 110 g for small piece, white. Steel crochet hook, size 0.90 mm.
FINISHED SIZE: Large 88 cm by 71 cm. Small: 43.5 cm by 71 cm. GAUGE: 10 cm = 20.5 spaces or blocks; 10 cm = 21 rows.

DIRECTIONS: For Small Chair Back: Ch 196 for foundation. Following chart, work 12 rows in filet crochet, increasing on both sides until there are 89 squares. Work even 137 rows in filet crochet, following chart. For Large: Make 2 small pieces and join as shown below.

Increasing and Joining

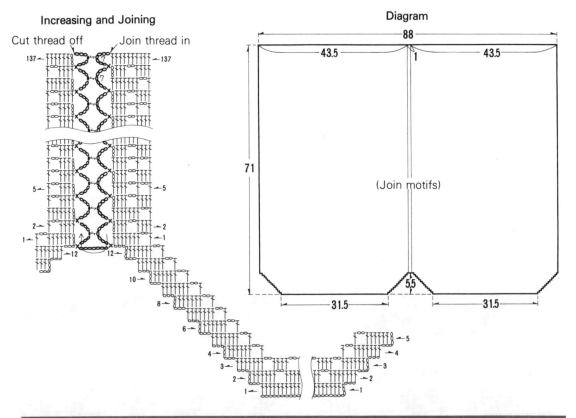

Diagram

Piano Cover, shown on page 25, bottom.

MATERIALS: Mercerized crochet cotton, No. 30, 400 g white. Steel crochet hook, sizes 0.90 mm and 0.75 mm.
FINISHED SIZE: 162 cm by 77.5 cm.
GAUGE: 10 cm = 22 rows; 10 cm = 22 spaces or blocks.
DIRECTIONS: Use 0.90 mm crochet hook except for last row which is worked with 0.75 mm crochet hook. * Ch 43 for foundation and work 4 rows, increasing on both sides. Repeat * 9 times. Join 2 pieces together (there are 5 joined pieces) and work 4 rows in filet crochet. Then work even 163 rows in filet crochet, following chart. Work sc all around.

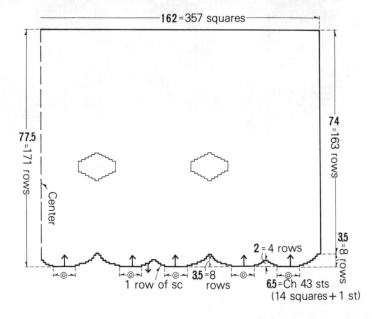

Cut thread off.

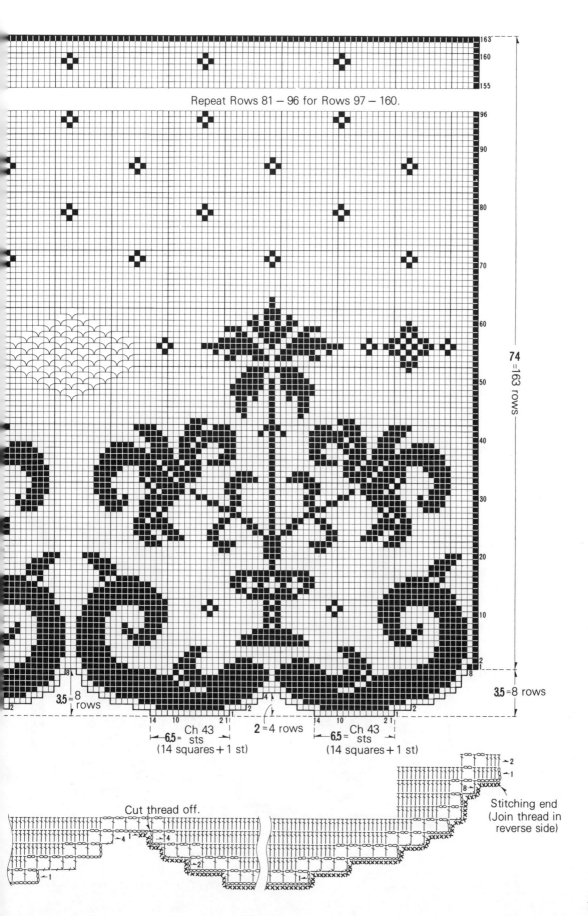

Repeat Rows 81 – 96 for Rows 97 – 160.

74 = 163 rows

3.5 = 8 rows

3.5 = 8 rows

Ch 43 sts
(14 squares + 1 st)

Ch 43 sts
(14 squares + 1 st)

2 = 4 rows

6.5 = sts

Cut thread off.

Stitching end
(Join thread in
reverse side)

MATERIALS: Mercerized crochet cotton, No. 30, 140 g white. Steel crochet hook, size 0.90 mm. White linen, 46 cm by 146 cm.
FINISHED SIZE: 143 cm by 29.5 cm (crocheted area).
GAUGE: 10 cm = 20.5 spaces or blocks; 10 cm = 23 rows.

DIRECTIONS: Ch 871 for foundation. Work 63 rows in filet crochet, following chart. Work edging all around, crocheting straight edge to linen.

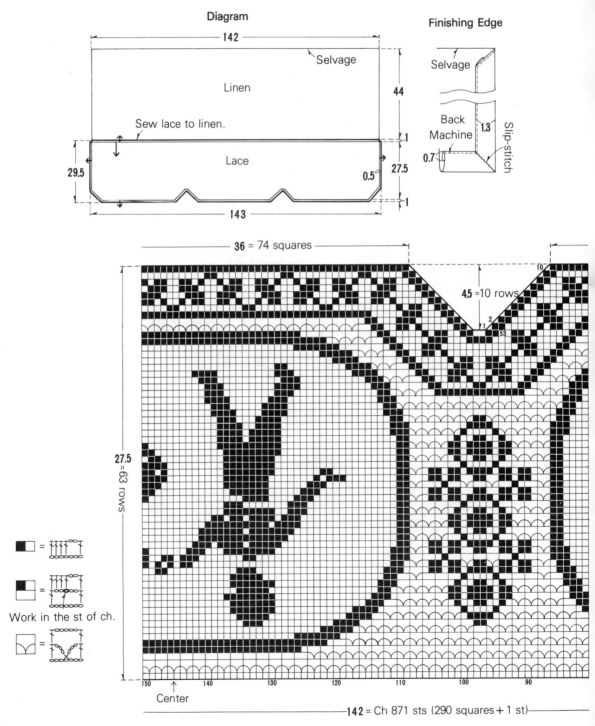

Diagram

Finishing Edge

142

Selvage

Linen

44

Sew lace to linen.

1.1

Lace

27.5

29.5

0.5

143

1

Selvage

Back Machine

1.3

Slip-stitch

0.7

36 = 74 squares

4.5 = 10 rows

27.5 = 63 rows

= Work in the st of ch.

Center

142 = Ch 871 sts (290 squares + 1 st)

Decreasing and Edging

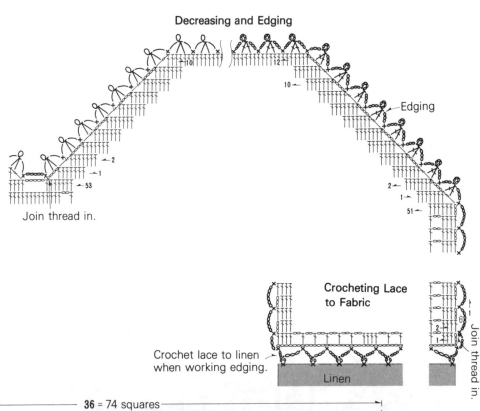

Join thread in.

Edging

Crocheting Lace to Fabric

Crochet lace to linen when working edging.

Linen

Join thread in.

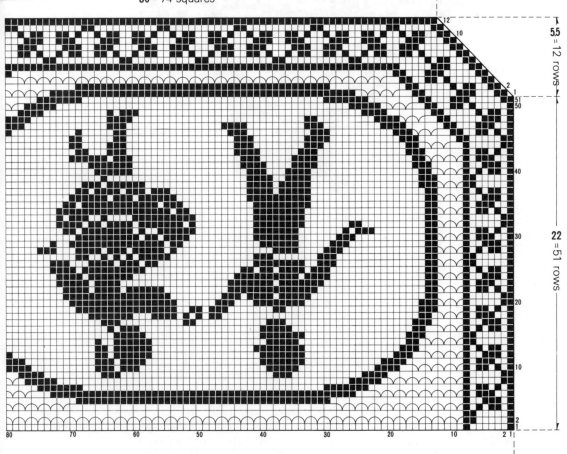

36 = 74 squares

5.5 = 12 rows

22 = 51 rows

MATERIALS FOR ONE PILLOW: Mercerized crochet cotton, No. 30, 140 g white. Steel crochet hook, size 0.90 mm. Red (navy) velveteen, 51 cm by 100 cm. Inner pillow stuffed with kapok, 50 cm square. Five white buttons, 1.2 cm in diameter.

FINISHED SIZE: 49 cm square.

GAUGE: 10 cm = 20 spaces or blocks; 10 cm = 20 rows.

DIRECTIONS: For Front: Ch 6, join with sl st to form ring. Rnd 1: Ch 3, dc 3, (ch 3, dc 4) 3 times, ch 1, end with h dc. Rnds 2−49: Work in filet crochet and lacet sts, following chart and increasing at corners. For Back: Ch 6, join with sl st to form ring. Rnd 1: Ch 3, (ch 3, dc 4) twice, ch 3, h dc 3, ch 3, end with sl st. Rows 2−38: Work in filet crochet and lacet sts, following chart and increasing at two corners. Turn every row and make left half. Make right half in the same way, following chart. Rnd 39: Place right hallf on left half, overlapping 2 dc sts crosswise. Work in filet crochet, following chart and joining tow halves. Rnds 40−48: Work following chart. Rnd 49: Work in filet crochet, joining to Front. Work in sc for opening of Back, making loops for button on right half. Make 49 cm square inner pillow with velveteen and stuff with kapok. Insert inner pillow into lace pillow.

Front

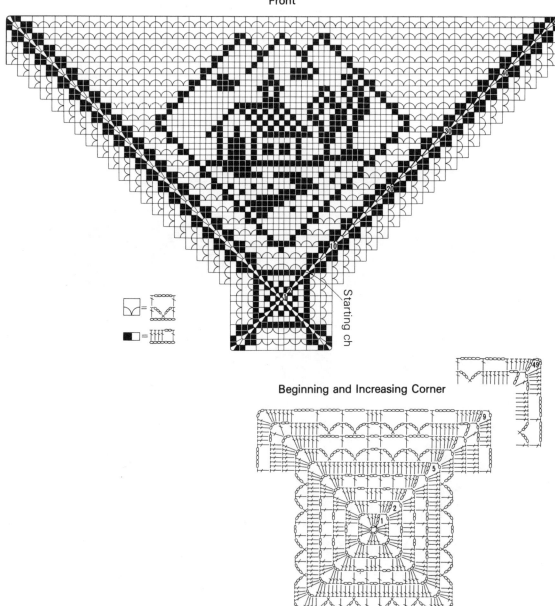

Starting ch

Beginning and Increasing Corner

Crocheting Back

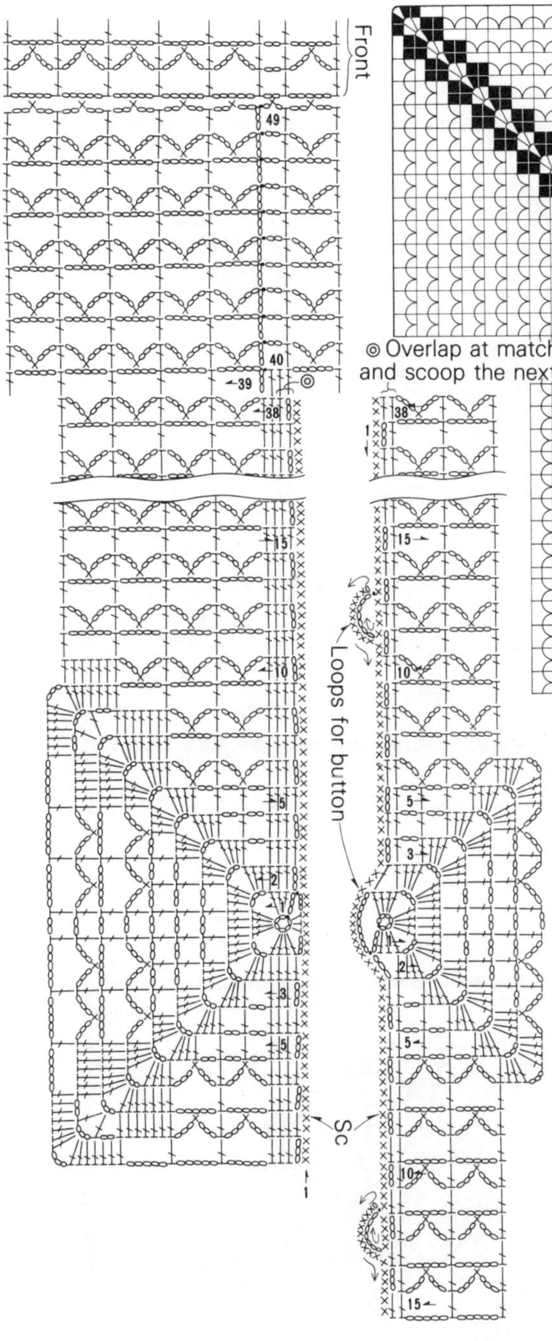

Front

Back

49

Front

49

40
←39 40 ◎
←39
←38 ◎ Overlap at matching mark,
38 and scoop the next row.

49

↑40
←39
←38

38←
35←

Loops for button

30←

25←

20←

1 row of Sc

15←

15

15

38

10

10

5←
3←

5

5
3

1←
2←

2
1

3←
5←

Loops for button

Loops for button

5←

3←

2

Sc

5←

1

10←

15←

77

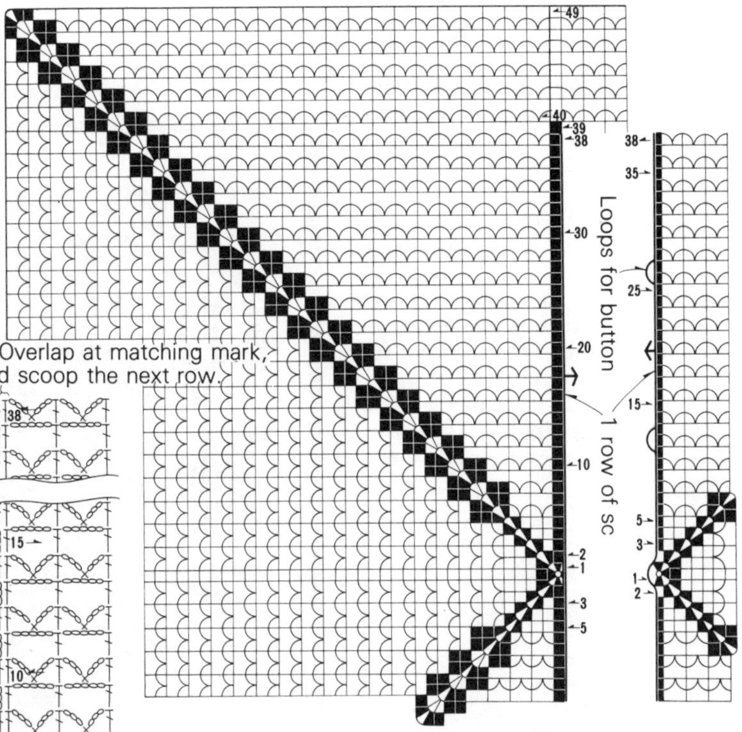

MATERIALS: Mercerized crochet cotton, No. 30, 1620 g white. Steel crochet hook, size 0.90 mm.

FINISHED SIZE: 259.5 cm by 177 cm.

SIZE OF MOTIF: 29 cm by 28.5 cm.

GAUGE: 10 cm = 20 spaces or blocks; 10 cm = 20 rows.

DIRECTIONS: To make motif, ch 175 for foundation. Work 57 rows in filet crochet, following each chart for motifs A, B, and C. Make required number of motifs. Join 9 motifs into a strip, following diagram. Then, join 9-motif strips together. work 4 rnd edging

A motif   Make 14 pieces.

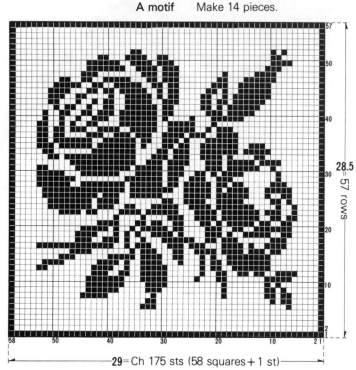

29 = Ch 175 sts (58 squares + 1 st)

28.5 = 57 rows

Diagram

B motif   Make 13 pieces.

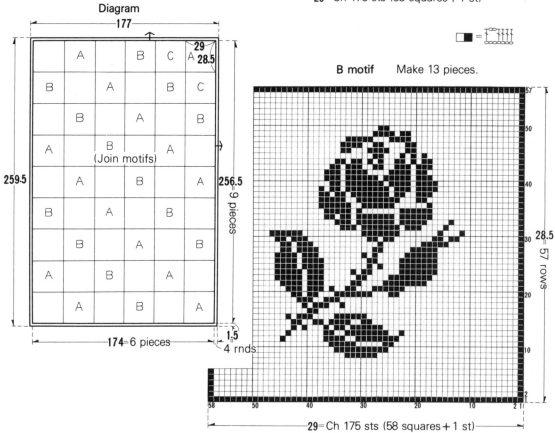

29 = Ch 175 sts (58 squares + 1 st)

28.5 = 57 rows

C motif　　Make 27 pieces.

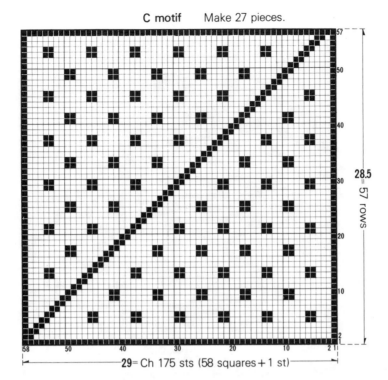

28.5 = 57 rows

29 = Ch 175 sts (58 squares + 1 st)

Joining Motifs and Edging

Sc in 7th st between motifs on top and botton edges.

6sts

Cut thread off.

Join thread in.

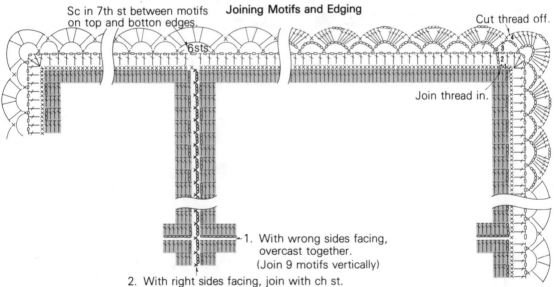

1. With wrong sides facing, overcast together. (Join 9 motifs vertically)
2. With right sides facing, join with ch st.

Boy and Girl Bedspread, shown on page 28.

MATERIALS: Mercerized crochet cotton, No. 30, 1150 g white. Steel crochet hook, size 0.90 mm.
FINISHED SIZE: 300 cm by 174 cm.
SIZE OF MOTIF: 40 cm aquare.
GAUGE: 10 cm = 18 spaces or blocks; 10 cm = 18.5 rows.

DIRECTIONS: To make motifs, ch 214 for foundation. Work 73 rows in filet crochet and lacet sts, following each chart for motifs A, B, and C. Make required number of motifs. Work edging (1) around motifs, joining 7 motifs by 4 motifs as shown in diagram. Work 3 rnd edging (2) all around. On 3rd rnd of edging, adjust (decrease) sts at center of each side.

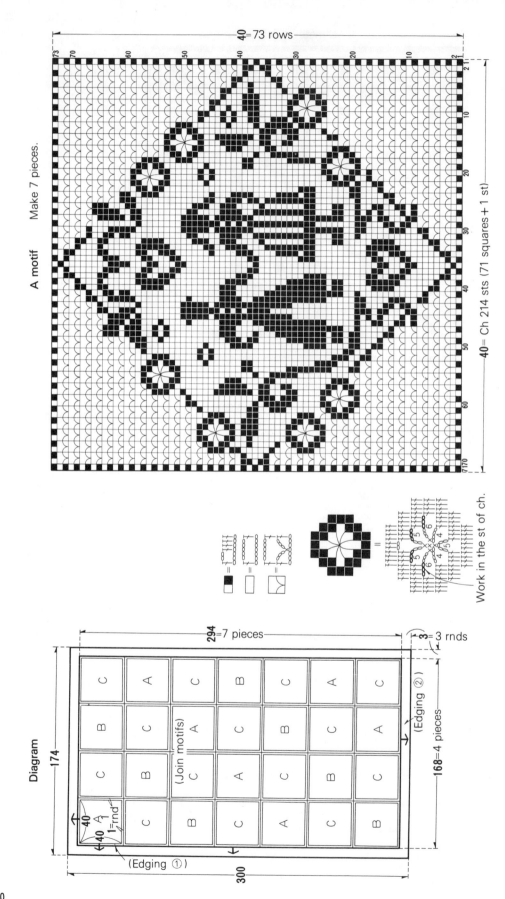

A motif   Make 7 pieces.

40 = 73 rows

40 = Ch 214 sts (71 squares + 1 st)

Work in the st of ch.

Diagram

294 = 7 pieces

3 = 3 rnds

174

168 = 4 pieces

300

(Edging ①)

(Edging ②)

(Join motifs)

40

1 = rnd

C motif   Make 14 pieces.

B motif   Make 7 pieces.

40＝73 rows

40＝Ch 214 sts (71 squares＋1 st)

40＝Ch 214 sts (71 squares＋1 st)

(Edging and Joining, Shown on next page.)

Edging and Joining

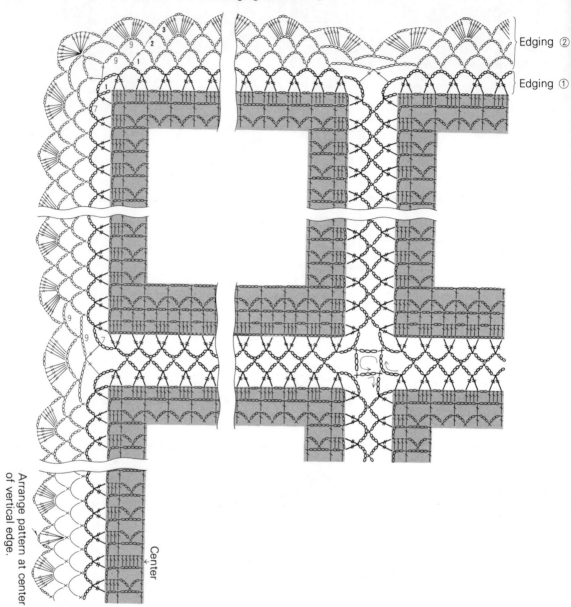

Edging ②

Edging ①

Arrange pattern at center of vertical edge.

Center

Lace Edging for Curtain, shown on page 29.

MATERIALS: Mercerized crochet cotton, NO. 30, 100 g white. Steel crochet hook, size 1.00 mm. White georgette crepe, 92 cm by 314 cm. Cotton tape, 5 cm by 184 cm. Slip-in hooks, 8. Pin-on hooks, 2.
FINISHED SIZE: Length, 163.5 cm. Width of lace, 8.5 cm.
GAUGE: 1 dc = 0.6 cm; 1 pattern (16 rows) = about 10 cm.

DIRECTIONS: Ch 31 for foundation. Work in filet crochet, following chart. Repeat Rows 2 — 17 (one pattern) until the piece reaches 366th row. Cut fabric as indicated and make side hem. Sew on cotton tape. Place lace edging on right side of fabric and sew in slip-stitch. Attach hooks. Make another symmetrical piece.

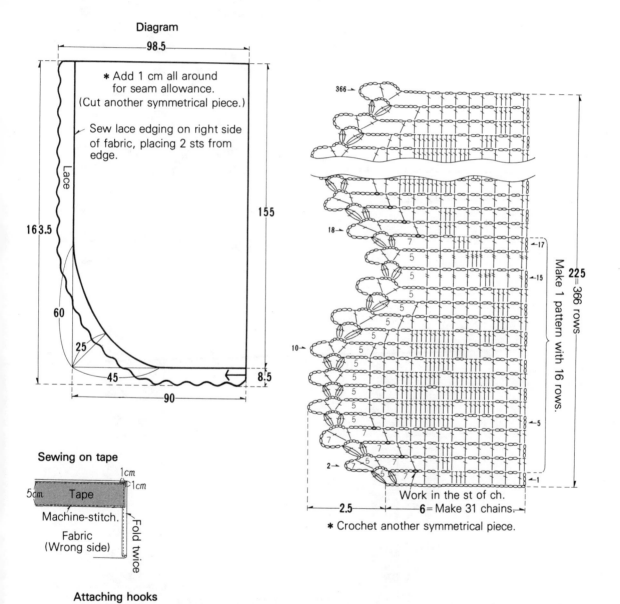

Diagram

Sewing on tape

Attaching hooks

MATERIALS: Mercerized crochet cotton, No. 30, 60 g light brown. Steel crochet hook, size 0.90 mm.
FINISHED SIZE: 54 cm by 28 cm.
SIZE OF MOTIF: 12 cm square.
GAUGE: 10 cm = 22 spaces or blocks; 10 cm = 22 rows.

DIRECTIONS: To make motif, ch 79 for foundation. Work 26 rows in filet crochet, following chart. Work one rnd in mesh pattern, joining motifs. Make and join 4 by 2 motifs. Work 2 rnd edging.

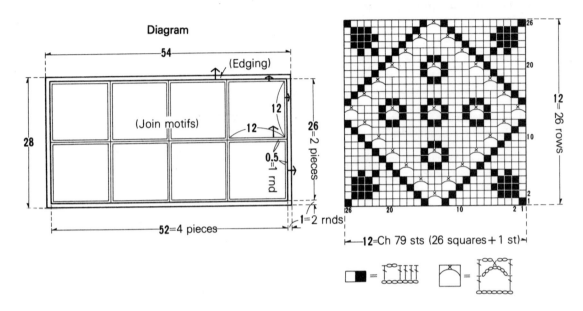

Diagram

Joining motifs and Edging

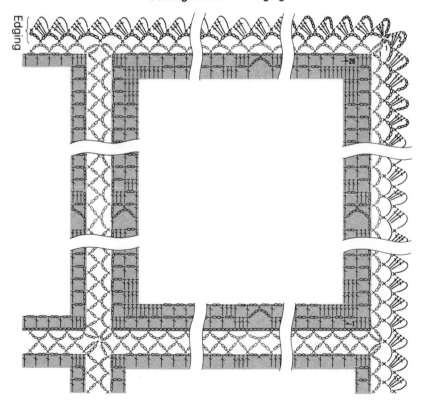

MATERIALS: Mercerized crochet cotton, No. 30, 45 g white. Steel crochet hook, size 0.90 mm.
FINISHED SIZE: 34.5 cm square.
GAUGE: 10 cm = 20 spaces or blocks; 10 cm = 20 rows.

DIRECTIONS: Ch 202 for foundation. Work 67 rows in filet crochet, following chart. Work 3 rnds in sc all around.

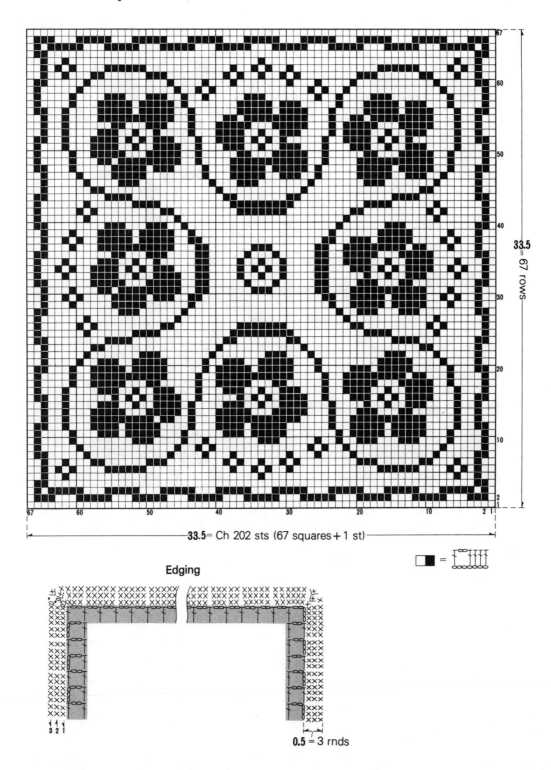

33.5 = 67 rows

33.5 = Ch 202 sts (67 squares + 1 st)

Edging

0.5 = 3 rnds

MATERIALS: Mercerized crochet cotton, No. 30, 45 g white. Steel crochet hook, size 0.90 mm.
FINISHED SIZE: 34 cm square.
GAUGE: 10 cm = 21 spaces or blocks; 10 cm = 21 rows.

DIRECTIONS: Ch 202 for foundation. Work 67 rows in filet crochet, following chart. Work 2 rnd edging. On 2nd rnd of edging make chain loop on every 6th st except at center.

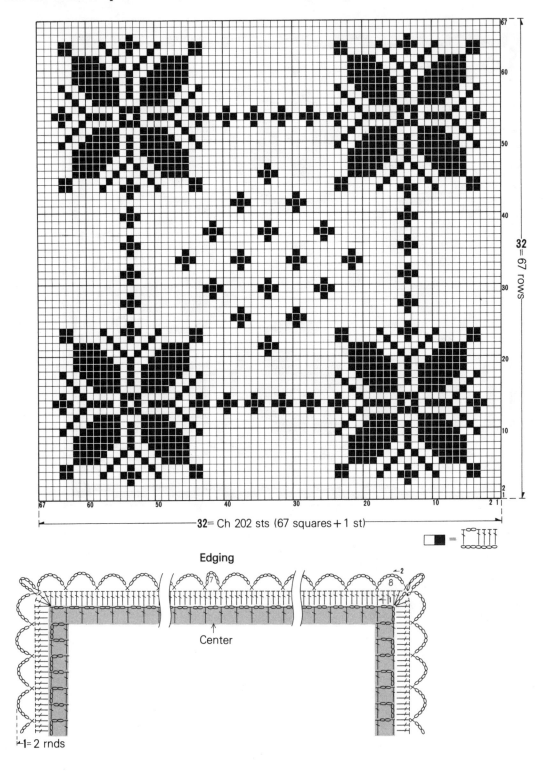

32 = 67 rows

32 = Ch 202 sts (67 squares + 1 st)

Edging

Center

1 = 2 rnds

Arrow Table Center, *shown on page 31, bottom.*

MATERIALS: Mercerized crochet cotton, No. 30, 70 g beige. Steel crochet hook, size 0.90 mm.

FINISHED SIZE: 63.5 cm by 38 cm.
GAUGE: 10 cm = 15 spaces or blocks; 10 cm = 14 rows.
DIRECTIONS: Ch 213 for foundation. Work 85 rows in filet crochet, following chart. Work 3 rnd edging.

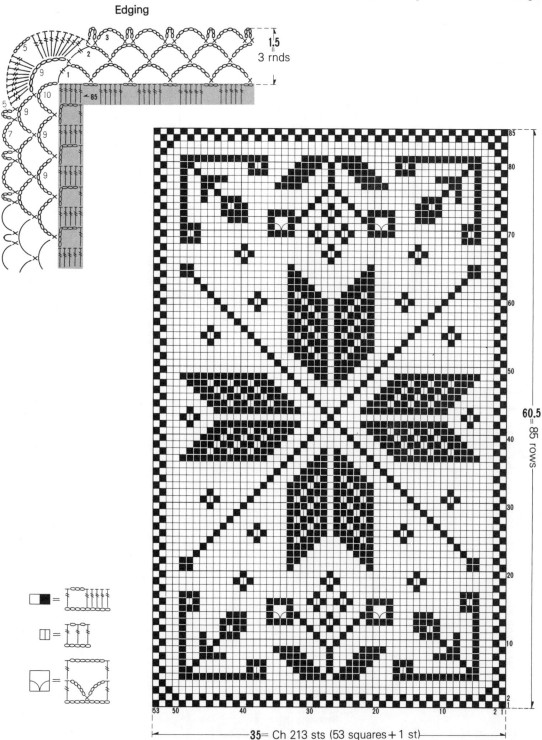

Edging

1.5 = 3 rnds

60.5 = 85 rows

35 = Ch 213 sts (53 squares + 1 st)

MATERIALS: Mercerized crochet cotton, No. 30, 150g beige. Steel crochet hook, size 0.90 mm.
FINISHED SIZE: 84.5 cm by 60.5 cm.
GAUGE: 10 cm = 15 spaces or blocks; 10 cm = 15 rows.
DIRECTIONS: Ch 61 for foundation. Rows 1–10: Work in filet crochet, following chart and increasing on both sides. Rows 11–59: Work even, following chart. Make 2 more pieces in the same way. Row 60: Work in sc, joining 3 pieces with 7 ch between them. Rows 61–81: Work in filet crochet, following chart. Work edging in sc and ch as shown. Make loops for hanging.

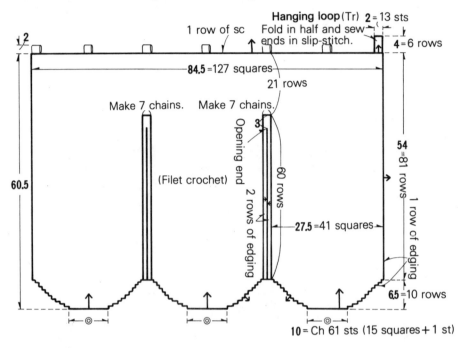

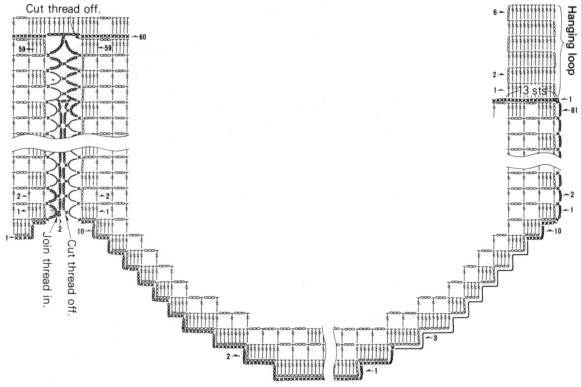

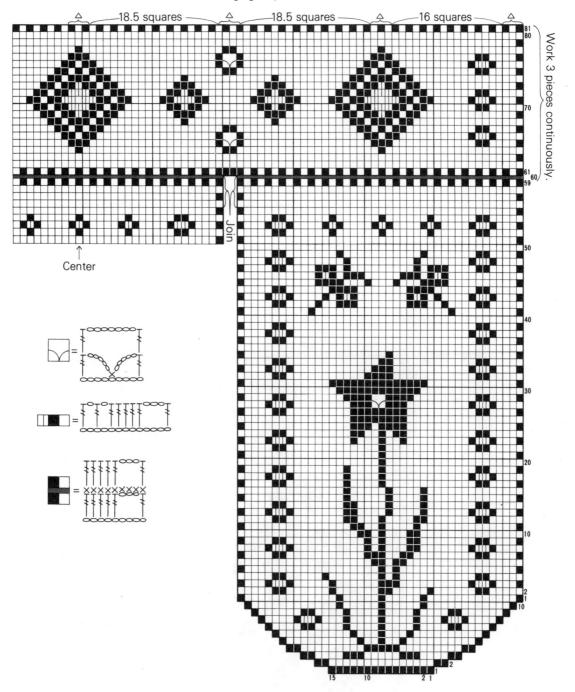

△ = Attach hanging loop here.

Tree Lace Curtain, *shown on page 32, bottom.*

MATERIALS: Mercerized crochet cotton, No. 30, 120 g white. Steel crochet hook, size 0.90 mm.
FINISHED SIZE: 85.5 cm by 35.5 cm.
GAUGE: 10 cm = 20.5 spaces or blocks; 10 cm = 20.5 rows.

DIRECTIONS: Ch 175 for foundation. Work 52 rows in filet crochet, following chart. Make 2 more pieces in the same way. Join 3 pieces together on Row 53 and work through Row 73. Make loops for hanging. Fold them in half and sew ends slip-stitch.

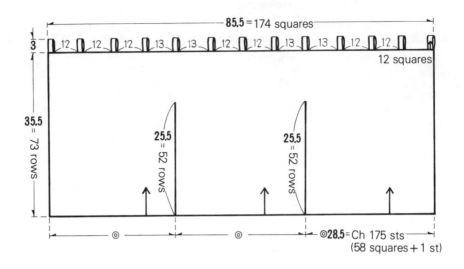

85.5 = 174 squares

3

12   12   12   13   13   12   12   13   13   12   12

12 squares

35.5 = 73 rows

25.5 = 52 rows

25.5 = 52 rows

©28.5 = Ch 175 sts
(58 squares + 1 st)

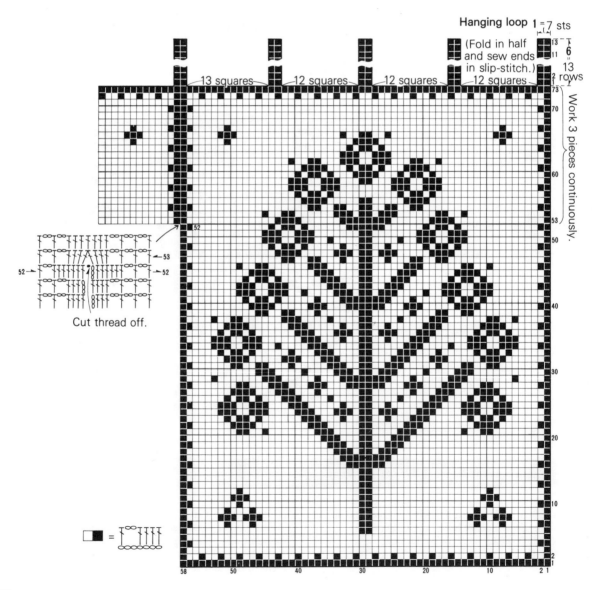

Hanging loop 1 = 7 sts

(Fold in half
and sew ends
in slip-stitch.)

13
11

6 = 13 rows

13 squares   12 squares   12 squares   12 squares

Work 3 pieces continuously.

Cut thread off.

To Begin

✿ Make chain and form ring.

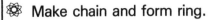

✿ Make loop.

1   **2**   **3**   **4**   **5**

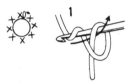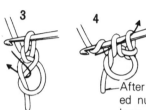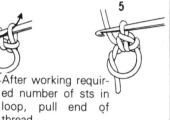

After working requir-
ed number of sts in
loop, pull end of
thread.

✿ To pick up sts through chain.

1   **2**   **3**   **4**

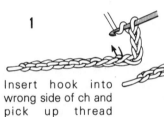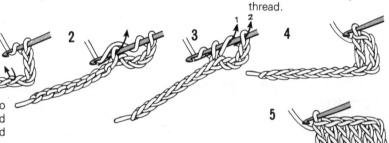

Insert hook into
wrong side of ch and
pick up thread
through ch.

5

Difference in Stitch Symbols

Note difference in stitch symbols for (a) and (b).

For (a), all sts are worked
over chain loop.

1   **2**

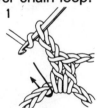

For (b), all sts are inserted
into ch.

1   **2**

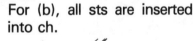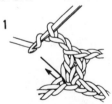

Starting or Turning Chain

On every row or round, st starting or turning a chain is counted as
one st except when sc. The stitch symbols at right show one ch st.
Sc is equal to one ch, hdc to 2 ch, dc to 3 ch, and so on. When
working round, end with sl st in top of starting ch of the rnd and
start ch again for next rnd.

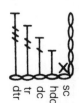

dtr   tr   dc   hdc   sc

HOW TO INC OR DEC IN FILET CROCHET

TO INCREASE

A

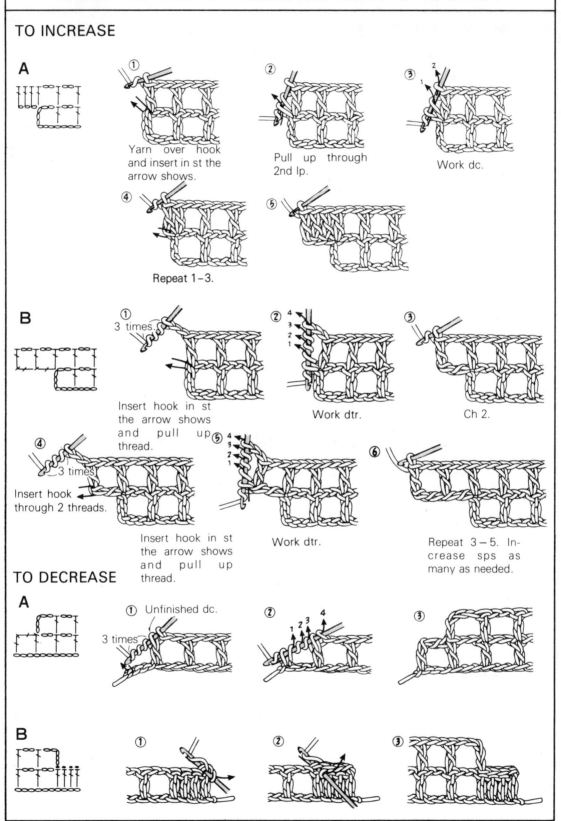

① Yarn over hook and insert in st the arrow shows.

② Pull up through 2nd lp.

③ Work dc.

④ ⑤ Repeat 1–3.

B

① 3 times. Insert hook in st the arrow shows and pull up thread.

② Work dtr.

③ Ch 2.

④ 3 times. Insert hook through 2 threads. Insert hook in st the arrow shows and pull up thread.

⑤ Work dtr.

⑥ Repeat 3 – 5. Increase sps as many as needed.

TO DECREASE

A

① Unfinished dc. 3 times

②

③

B

①

②

③

HOW TO JOIN MOTIFS

A: Join with drawn-out thread by re-inserted hook.

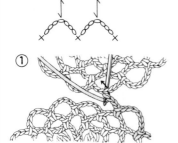

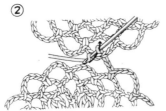

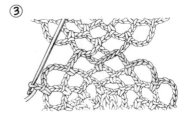

Drop lp from hook. Insert hook in sp of net, pick up dropped lp, and pull up through net.

Continue working in ch.

B: Join with sl st.

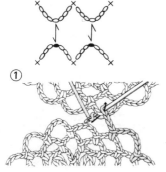

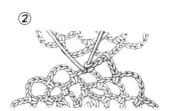

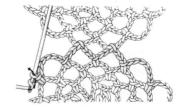

Insert hook in net.
Pull up thread through net.

C: Join with sc.

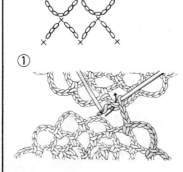

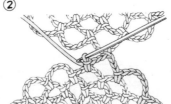

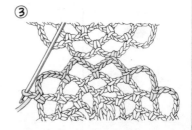

BASIC CROCHET STITCHES

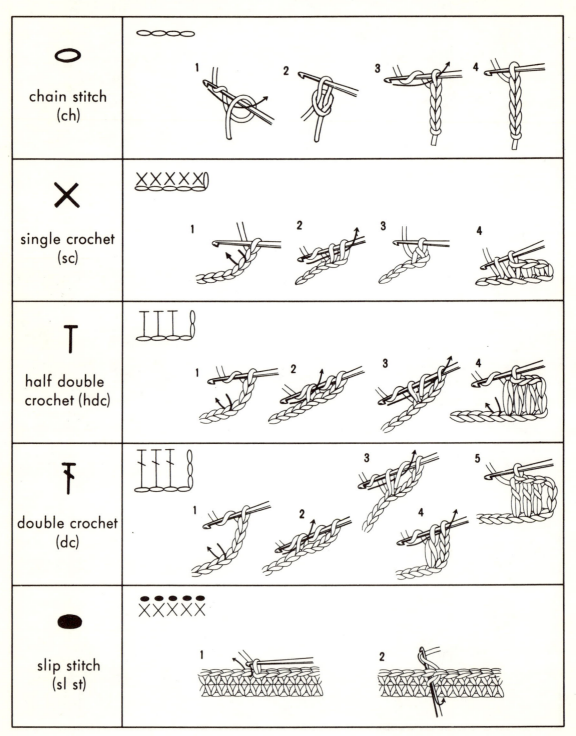

chain stitch (ch)	
single crochet (sc)	
half double crochet (hdc)	
double crochet (dc)	
slip stitch (sl st)	

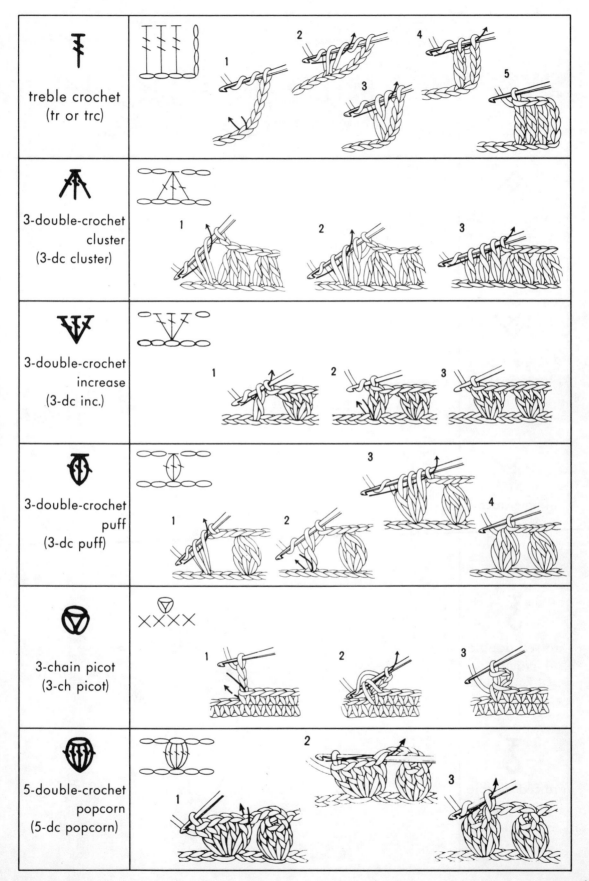

treble crochet (tr or trc)		
3-double-crochet cluster (3-dc cluster)		
3-double-crochet increase (3-dc inc.)		
3-double-crochet puff (3-dc puff)		
3-chain picot (3-ch picot)		
5-double-crochet popcorn (5-dc popcorn)		

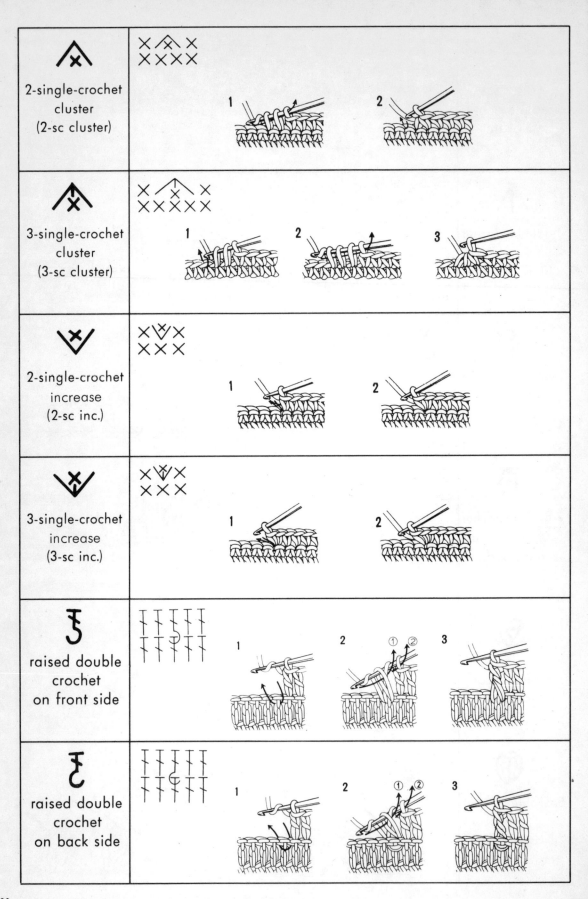

2-single-crochet cluster (2-sc cluster)		
3-single-crochet cluster (3-sc cluster)		
2-single-crochet increase (2-sc inc.)		
3-single-crochet increase (3-sc inc.)		
raised double crochet on front side		
raised double crochet on back side		